LIFE CONTEMPLATED

FREE VERSE FROM INCARCERATION

MALKIESE PAYTHRESS

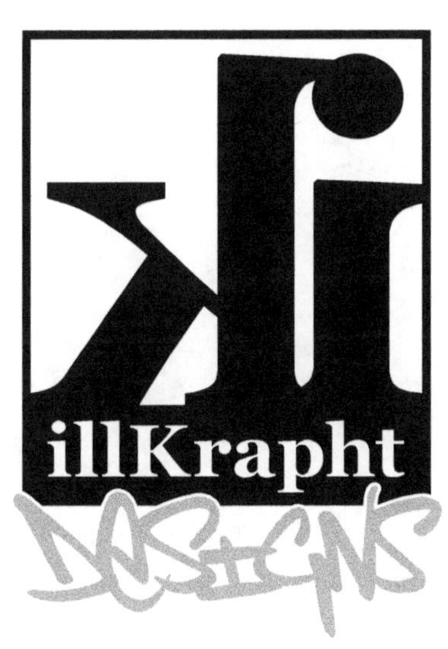

ART CREATION IS THE DOCUMENTATION OF THE SOUL'S VOICE

Life Contemplated: Free Verse From Incarceration
All artwork, poems, design and layout by M. Paythress
illKrapht Paythress Publishing- Cleveland, Ohio

http://www.visualcv.com/paythressillkrapht
https://www.facebook.com/m.paythress

ISBN 978-0-9916531-1-9

Life Contemplated is a collection of free verse poetic writings that was put together while incarcerated at various correctional facilities around Ohio. Different art forms come alive in my mind when I flow inside the magic of creating. Hopefully, any visitors to my world can appreciate the work before them. Please stay healthy, safe and FREE!

To all my family, I love you all...

Other titles from Malkiese Paythress

Will Someone Get My Damn Bond!!

Abstrak Urban Consep2all Poetik

CONTENTS

CONTEMPLATED

MEDITATED

REFLECTED

CONTEMPLATED

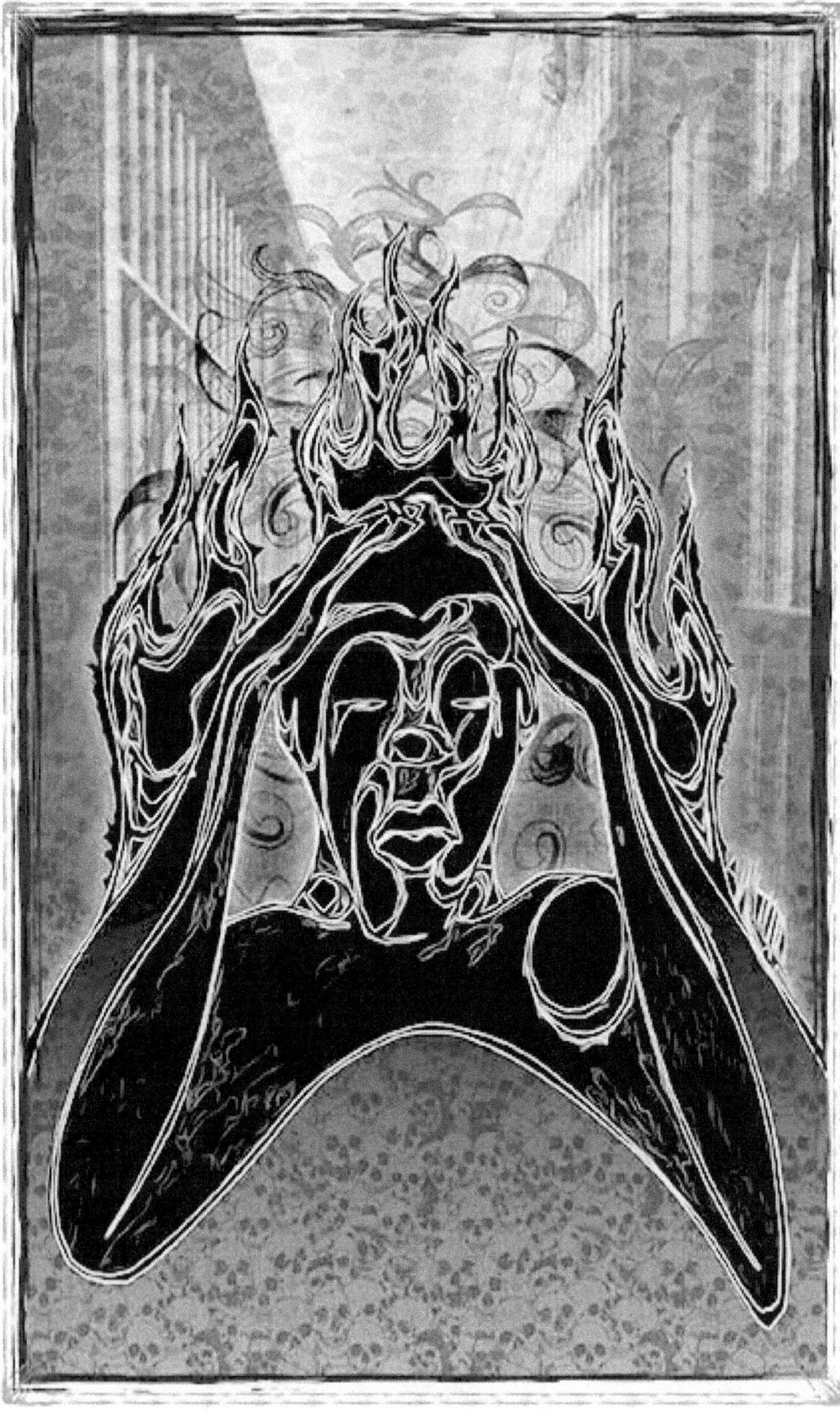

LIFE CONTEMPLATED

Contemplating life's future goals
How to cope middle aged
reaching for an achievement
that should've been made years ago
working with mental health as an issue
approaching it like there's only despair
in the smog filled air of a drowning society
dealing with forms and thoughts of emotions regularly
infatuated with the melodic tone of deliverance
that spoken word brings
needing ways to make time pass more effortlessly
wanting the nostalgia that can't be broken
by one or two slips of the spirit
only complemented by the soulful
next step to the drum
better yet humdrum
and be content that I can soul clap
and still write to that
wondering where thoughts are gonna lead me to next
trying not to collapse in spirit
wearily waiting for a solution
What can all the labor in life bring?
future uncertain
What's next to nurture and grow?
as if having children doesn't leave
work cut out for a grown man
I suppose make sure their blessings come in multiples
with that in mind
please excuse me while I kick in every door of opportunity
until I can get a strong hold with perseverance
to a prosperous plane
clutching my essential lane space and domain

WITH ENUFF PAPER

With fifty pages to write
I can plot a revolution
and have the coup documented
But what would happen if I get caught?
more hole time with a need for a lawyer
to justify my behalf
Can I stand the drama?

With enuff paper
I could make airplanes to fly for months
and still be able to flush them all away
Wouldn't that be fun?
BUT WHY?

The pages I document thoughts on
could be scoffed at yet still
my points are made as I write
it took me a while to learn to organize
these groups of letters pronounced
time spent just in thought
of what to put back together

I dissected my mind and placed it again
for the sake of poetry
sometimes I don't even grasp what I do
with fifty pages to document the eventful experience
to share with the reading, listening public

With a notepad of paper just to set it
please, these fifty pages are for me to vent
releasing my frustration to the blank whiteness
that is now the canvas for letter and voice painting
satisfied at the end
becuz when I'm finished
I've created something

REMEMBER YOUR KIDS

Son is healthy with all his digits
in good working order
and yet...

Even with that blessing
my beautiful, strong, baby boy
with a vivid character and clever ways
has escaped my mind so many...
probably too many times
while I spend isolation time
in jive about my writings

What does that say about me?
at that though...
now I have a newborn and married
into the responsibility of two more
an older son and daughter
proven more self sufficient
and living with a kinder world outlook
both to be noteworthy goal achievers

When I stop and reflect
these kids were more an influence on me
growing into college educated life
before I even had a chance to finish
though I stepped with a head start years ago

My gray mustache hairs and prison number
make me think twice before giving advice
to these kids...
who are obviously more in tune
with this society than me
ME, ME, me...

Hope these kids grasp their importance to the future
a whole genealogy was blessed with their coming
and presence...
a person can sense it in their smiles

With honesty
and honestly seeing the new millennium
gift of wit that
older and younger generations can learn from
bleeding with talent
hopefully becoming polished enuff to remain humble

Learning to cope
having an outpouring of wisdom
in all complex situations
the world is constantly getting more violent
but you kids are surviving
throughout the breakdowns and arguments

I can't speak for all parents becuz it isn't my position
but I knew you children were built to last
when we became a family
if I ever come off too harsh or tough
it's only becuz I remembered
and hopefully it all just reinforces your solid structure

There is no drama that you can't overcome
no matter how nasty or outlandish
I know I'm not the best example
but I know to believe
that you'll be better than me

Hopefully better off than the environments
my limited life has allowed you to see
bless your life and learn from the mistakes
you've known in me
ME, ME, me...

I should've taken more time to help you build
and maybe you should see me as a selfish individual
but even so...

I'm glad you're part of ME, ME, me...

However corny that may seem
get you blushing
or even angry
there's a strong possibility that you're in my life
to be examples to me...
and truthfully that is just what I needed!

AWAITING A DATE OF RELEASE

I spent almost a year
hoping for the best
expecting the worst
and knowing the negative...

Defensive about every aspect otherwise...

Then I walked into the courtroom
and my sentence came
it came from the mouth
that I knew was going to lash at me
and address me as a career criminal

As a matter of fact
the judge's teeth chattered just that in a sense...
surprisingly enuff though

I wasn't stroked with an ear-popping amount of time
my few years given with a chance to appeal
and open still for judicial release
might piss a few heads off

Wanting utmost punishment
but my time motivated more writing

You still reading?
Or listening to the words whistle?

Poetry once again my release and medium of messaging
the thought of accomplishing something
is once again alive in my head

Moving my pen to document
where my thought trains
brainwaves and constant flow concerning
my viewpoint on my situation left off to...

For the time released from darkness slightly
with my case finishing up I'm still tense
my relief might jinx me on my journey
I haven't forgot how close the drama sticks to me

So even still, I don't expect to be fully happy
steady wondering where my next hole shot is coming from
and what lesson it'll bring
hopefully I can stay calmer next time around
seeing how I'm now in my thirties
awaiting my date of release

TO GET EN ROUTE

Wide awake
it's the middle of the night
thinking my next move had better get me right
it better be legit
and I had better be able to maximize
after my attitude adjustment

I'm now thinking super-sized
soberly
coping more humbly
goal oriented and viewed as sane
with my presented self thankfully...

My next civilian appearance should show
a more polished side of me
that's for even your benefit
as well as the rest of society
that's how it's supposed to be
Now I'll say it's safe to quote me

Am I acting too quickly?
A little too soon?

My get up is always a little fast
that's definitively me
self-sacrifice was paid with overtime
and multitasking...

My journey still has me on a long trek ahead
and it's now time for my second wind to come
as people come and go
with even more time and space to pass
more grind acquired and my next venture
BETTER REFLECT IT!

This, that and the other won't matter much anymore
if I can't hold steady to a clean success
notes taken to become a noteworthy individual
should not get the soul pressed or negatively anxious
let me simply remember this with these writings
as they build and destroy in the process of aiding self-renovation
and help me be more about action than idle talking
not a downfall or ditch to be stuck in

As I prepare to walk a destined path to success... AGAIN...

DO MY THING

Quiet and out of sight as the time goes by
contemplate success while everybody else glances and passes by
busy in their own lives
how to maximize what I put forth in energy and time
is now what makes moves come in perpetual motion
my plays towards success are now what occupy my mind
they have to be, my aim is to be goal oriented
too gifted to let it all go to waste
or let any little bit of talent be spilled
without it being soaked back up to be used in a mosaic
I THINK I CAN, I KNOW I CAN
and roll in first person still staying in agreement
with whatever's listening
and my goal's gonna still get accomplished

A PROCESS OF REARRANGING THE OUTPUT OF MY OWN FRICTION

Steady self-supply the power grid and own it
I know now there is enuff of me coming to do this
rock with me if you will
but remember I don't stand as the teacher
I am more like the note taking student
never mind the glamour
let me stick to the maintenance of foundations
stay working to keep everything solid
I've collapsed before
it's not as easy or pretty as an experience
but it is a relief to be able to rebuild from it though
there is no need to wear it on my sleeve
wipe my sweat from my brow
and get back to my comfort zone of working
I've learned that many times over
balance is more stable when you hands on DROP BOMBS
blue-collar fatigue and work ethic
at that more independent just getting done what needs to be done
now putting to use my documented ideas
instead of idle talking about the other and this

There's a duty in staying focused and I've noticed
poetics help to grasp the rhythmical movement of motion waves
whether sound, light or heat
all towards a destination
a thought train followed by physical action is a powerful thing
it has built countries and changed multimillion people strong regimes by revolution
and more work gets done when there is no one to fool and no one fooling
hustle and grind

I speak of self when I say and be about putting B.S. to the side
all of that and no more worries about being ALL THAT
if something ain't right involving me
let me shut up and fix it
openly blessed enuff to do this
coped with both losses and achievements

Learning...

I'm not a masochist, I enjoy the achievements more
not a heavy drinker
so stifle the next round call out for bloody Mary
and her drunk existence
no more acting like I need pitfalls
hold it down and remember all this
make something positive from it
letting cats go if they can't accept the vision
that's straightforward
don't step on toes
knowing there's multiple interpretations
all along the grand scheme of things and compass leans
towards individual perceptions
all in all, let me roll like I'm with it
critique ain't bothered me
but don't take me as ultra-naïve
acceptance grabbing from what the next man chooses to see
I'm already adjusted and tuned in to a personal route of energy
relatively fitted custom
my own cooking and preparation time fixed into a proper course of A to B
and I do apologize if I disrupted
stopping along my self-made scenic journey...

I thought I was trespassing so I had to acquire the property under foot
so please excuse me...
doing my thing

HOLE SHOT COSMONAUT

One small step for mankind
another leap achieved towards a hole shot
with handcuffs on and goon squad C.O.'s
manhandling my being and property
less than 24hrs since writings about a new outlook
were bleeding from my ink pen
I'm arguing with corporals and lieutenants
off to see the wizard of isolation again
not even a week since being sentenced
no love or respect
held my temper the best I can
trying to keep from swinging
and catching an assault on a C.O.
best believe the officers made it tempting
with all the name calling
ignited by their cell bogart
walking up hard

on a man minding his own business...

but ain't nobody hearing that
damn...
just forget it...
I'm off to my meds
a cosmonaut off in orbit
just pack my bible
socks
notepad
pen
put the cuffs on
I didn't want any problems
but I could tell by the look in the officer's eyes
he did...

Hell of a way to start my bid
but by now, I'm used to it
I've been waiting near a year
to catch distance from Cuyahoga county incarceration
and now that my trial is over
they can't stop that time from coming
threats of more charges prevail at nothing
they already think I'm crazy
I have no need to amuse and prove it
it's sad to know now that as an inmate
these officers need to try to keep a lingering incarceration
that's how they feed their children
but mine gotta eat too
plus my baby is gonna need a proper education

So I suppose...

As long as my date of release isn't getting lengthened and distanced
let me chill in the single cell given
mind my money moves
coordinate my civilian plans more
and relax jackin' to my freaky thoughts of women!
becuz the county jail still ain't talking about NUTHIN
and I'm still an unforgiven
hence, 23 and a half more hours of social darkness
contemplating the needed upkeep to a physical addiction
to popping psyche meds, just to keep my time coasting

Gotta let it all go
ignore the smart assed comments from the C.O.
and continue to float clear headed through artistic output
though, no matter other people's anger or mine
I'm about to roll to my parent institution
and the solution to my problems ain't with what they told
learning this firsthand
I guess that's for the soul and the glow

Do they even know?

If not, then..
LIKE I SAID
LIKE I SAID...
leave me the hell alone...

I ain't worried about the corporal's stripes
I GOT MY OWN
no matter what rights the courts strip
I am a man
and that won't change if another don't respect the fact
word for the day
marinate
the others...
cell therapy
hold my anger back before more drama spills
and I'm charged in another physical attack
I just know the courts and A.P.A. would be loving that
and I can't do nothing but yawn at another day in a cell
living just like that

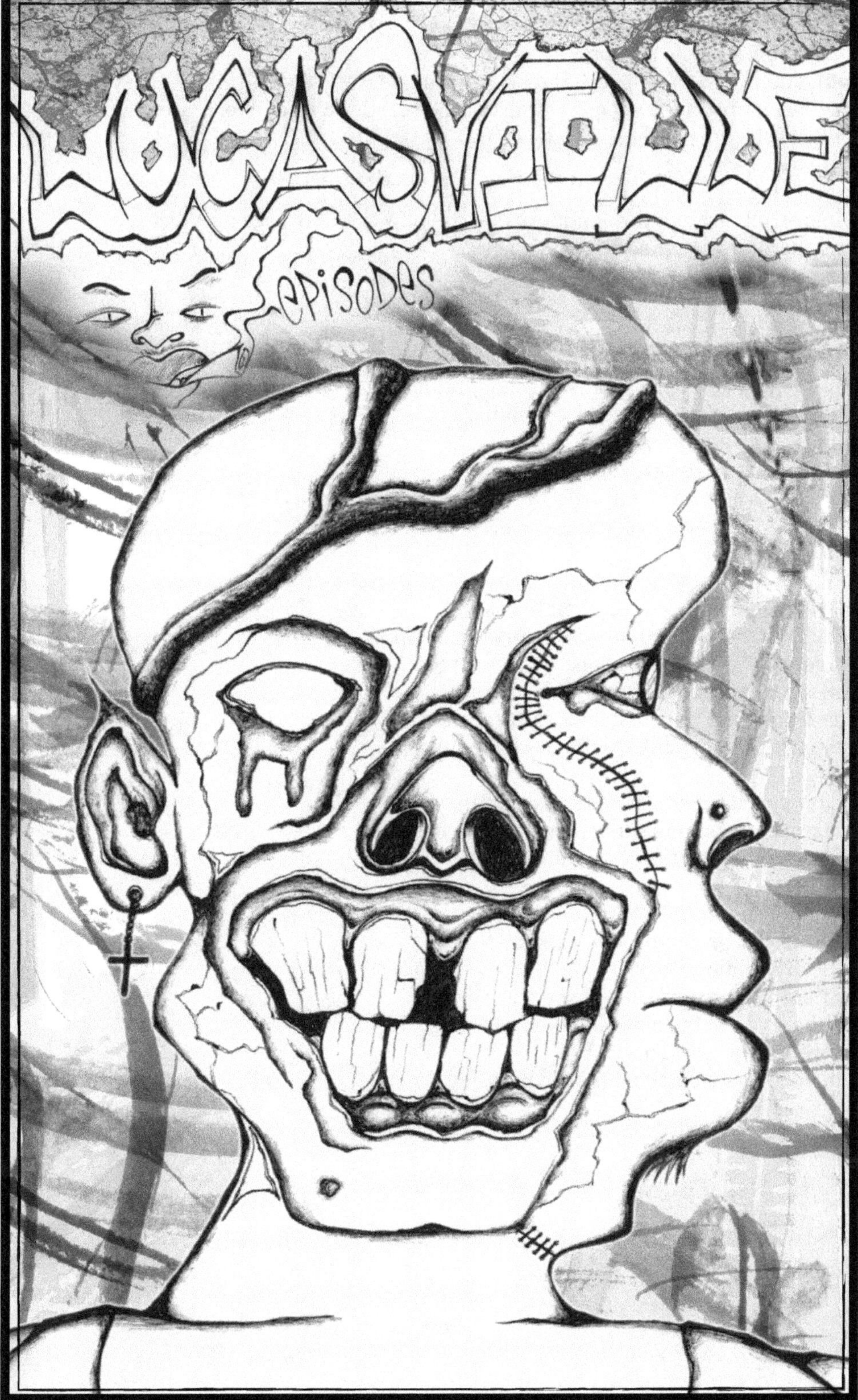
episodes

BOOGIE MONSTER

Time moving, slow motion
with enuff work in as a certified boogie monster
meeting a prison for a second time doesn't breed the term effervescence
for the self-professed cell block veteran
limp dick swinging
off tilt stagger
pimp stroll through the corridors that are now familiar with my voice
and thanks to tangling with turn keys
my blood and spit

An obvious menace to mainstream lifestyle, so now
I'm forced to cope with prison blues and state shoes
my tale just telling my excuse for not graduating
with the rest of my college freshman class
almost mid-thirties now
sitting back in a slow pause
so I can use the calm stillness to re-adjust my game's style

If it had any...

Now when the police run their checks
they'll find a certified boogie monster
ex-convict veteran to violence on the streets
I'm sober enuff to know now
that's not what the public needs to receive
nor is it what my child needs to believe in

So though sometimes the job search and career build
makes a grown man's independent living seem like
a distant dream at times

Nonstop as a man
chin up and protected as I walk on
mile after mile
until my dignity and self-respect is achieved
on the level that is mutually honored
by me and any criticizer until...
I'm no longer a certified boogie monster

WHAT THE THOUGHT BROUGHT

I'm writing while I'm overhearing talk of erotica on T.V.
for me, it's been nearly two years since I've even touched my woman

What does she smell like?
How does she taste?
my thoughts like...

It'll be another few years before
I can walk like a free man with one on my arm

As time goes on...
my interest in things to do for enjoyment slow down
my age moves on though...

2 yrs. ago, I needed to be with a woman
for nothing more than making love
now I would like to walk my lady through a park
full of the flowers she likes

Hopefully my attentions more focused
on the things that breed a solid relationship
a slow summer of love that can melt a woman
like ice cream on an Arizona summer day

Absolutely radiating feeling of companionship
strong affection for the one who is captivating your time
making the foundation complete
for the circle of intertwined life, love locked

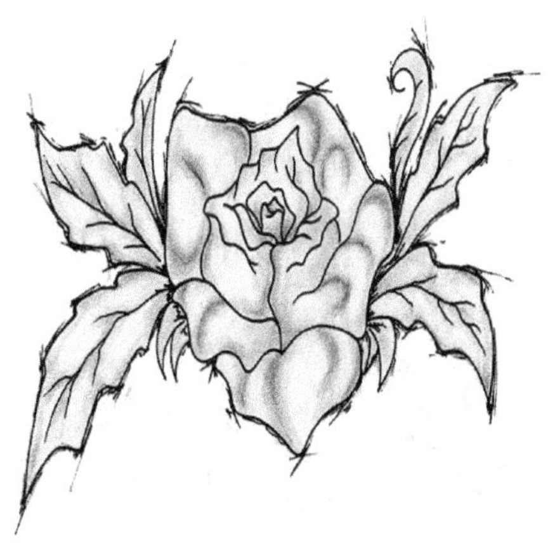

TAINTING MADE BOUNDARIES

P.S.

I was made aware of volunteer opportunities
although my arrest sheet made them unavailable to me
ceiling cap to what I can achieve
depression writings first hand
make the path I'm heeding and headed
sounded and seen
no longer a need to speak over beats
and study others in the similar mix'

That's like biting and trying to emulate another's cookie recipe
But who in general public gave a damn?
with all these amusement parks and carnivals so close range...

Zoning...
my mind flares kite
without a loss for words until my second coming

second pause...

Women's Heaven All Truth
a phrase I used to say before I woke up and realized
I had no job skills in a middle-aged time frame
minimum interaction with what some look for

That being...
retirement planning
away from weed plants and fire/paper mixtures
tainting the white picket fence dream
teaming supreme with luxury class suits and ties
an image that most want to get photo-flashed
How ya living?
over here, still existing unforgiven

TA AIM SOLID

Legal work, slow goings for me
living in a world wanting to curse my presence over money lust
hording
pack rat fear highlighted
when they can't complete it
their whole existence in business goes sour
trying to play understanding
to the left and prosecutor favors

I'm continually facing years
from intertwined so called dealers of my hand
side seat driving
back seat holla
backstabbers
some want a little too much
in a crazy world

So as gently as a strong-arm gets...

I hold redemption moves
while heads fiendin' for the other side of the game
hope for a footstep
cry wolf when the ankle breaks
and their hold to me slips
tripping from their own loose grip

My sense of self is solid
with freedom innately placed

Containment from an overseer
trying to gain power and dominance
because the way my name rolls off her tongue
probably won't get the true recognition it deserved

You don't want and can't have my triple life
sentenced from the spark of my verse

The first one
with no second guessing in my stanza delivery

AS TIME DRIFTS

As time drifts about its way
What is there to do?
mind-boggling
as I brainstorm, finishing my LC bid time
I would make a calendar but...
that sho' nuff slows time down
and I need ways to speed it up

Forget a distant out date for now
as I'm stuck overhearing arguments with C.O.'s
about the right to take a shower
along with mumblings about dinner

Thinking to myself

Should I open the new pack of playing cards I have
and get at a good game of solitaire?

Zoning like...
Who cares that I haven't called
or written to my family in months
I don't need the potential arguments
about petty things that could be
handled properly without my input

In other words
I'm not needed in correspondence

How about I take a home study course
in keeping up with my imagination
instead of perpin' like nothing's changed
now that I'm divorced and locked up

Artistic output has always been a good cover up
for anti-socialness and disdain
for the outside world
god bless the fact that I'm saved
and have no real addiction
to the hardcore street life that others portray

As real represents, is all that needed?
Maybe?

But I know for certain
it ain't for me to be a thug represent
of a prison system
so...

I should make sure to show polish
more so than grit

As well as...
make sure that as the reader reads
the words reflect it even through
the melancholy that I express with

Feel free to slide away if the words I gathered
don't fit a thing
ending like another non-attachment
writings added on to more writings
that aren't even deep and I realize
this page doesn't crack the shell of me

Not like the judicial
I know that did
indeed walking calmly away from first person
to blend with the masses
it's needed and justified
life's lessons are at a cost

Sometimes a crack of the whip is good by itself
other times it has to be followed by gunshots
something will be used to put a man back in line
and that force will be remembered
even if not acknowledged

How hard a force is based on stubbornness
and hope that a person can retain a slave's lesson
that is why it's given
it's important to remember the terms
rehabilitation and ***correction***
but is it all not punishment?

As time drifts by
my mind not so boggled
in a release of energy

If the thoughts can't be described as anything else

UNTITLED

Sometimes a man shouldn't express himself so much
especially if he has a tendency to be destructive
in naturally civil environments

But that doesn't mean he shouldn't be allowed to express at all

Spending time loving someone that destruction favors
is always hard

Always hard for the non-destructive party involved
Where goes the cherished thought of togetherness?
Was it falsely built?

That togetherness is the ballpoint joining
keeping the smoothness in the relationship
sometimes a fiery entity has to be spot-checked
and reminded of all that

It's hard to live in the calm
even for another's sake
when all you know is storm waves inside

At high tide
Will and can she tolerate the storm cloud's development?
more to the point...
Can she diffuse it?

All the destruction isn't meant for her
she seems to stay conveniently in the hurricane's path though

Maybe it takes a gentler
eloquent soul to make her aware of that
ace is high
but it feels too much like
there are jokers in the deck
as wild card style trumps
ego and disagreement
sour dealings to any relationship

Disarray can hopefully be worked out eventually
spending time loving someone that needs to be
by a man's side especially if he can't truly bare the turmoil

She needs to be acknowledged as a strong support
not belittled as part of the problem
hopefully love is strong enuff to work itself out
and conquer all
hopefully that love is mutually realized
as a two way street
with a meeting ground in peace
harmony
contentment
and enjoyable fulfillment...

ATTACKING WORDS SOBERLY

This time around, I step on the scene clean soberly
there is no inebriation to taint my navigation
attacking words and phrases...
soberly

No slurred speech when I speak these stanzas
and besides...

How can I maintain (even in written)
with a good foot?
and not be a truly tightened up soul
on step with a wide awake view to my outlook
no sense in being half cooked

Lushly living when I approach with my opinion
Who needs it from me?
I'm already viewed as an aggressive schizophrenic on cue
I have the credentials to back it if I needed them

Now let me refrain from picking up a bottle
before I sit down to explain why
I mean it this time as the verse tangents
with a slight whisper still of relevance
to the original matter of clean
sober functioning needed in this day and age

Neatly...

With an ace up my sleeve
adjusting nicely is how I feel about
coming into my next stage of life
without my recognizable stench of stale 40oz breath

Now the newly clearheaded is ready
to take his deserving spot of a polished man
on his own throne in his own rightful time

As his life repositions to complement a new found respect
for a more purified mind state

ME CROSSINGMINE

I'm spending life's time knowing
it's all mine and my product
no time for guilt or sorrow
What's next on the agenda for this adventure?
I met my oneness and greeted it this time around
a couple of years ago
I recognized it and disregarded
try not to downgrade the elusive move away
from peace and average contentment
I meant the best for the world
when I choose to sidestep INI
knowing I could still bring destruction
How does that sound from a self-proclaimed ruthless child?
pausing motion so long
only to inhale the distant scent
of an everlasting wars' mushroom cloud
I'm at ease in a state of
continually leaving others in shock
it's either that or face up to the fact that
no one opposes me all the time
I'm just paranoid of being mocked
for that, no one jocks or lobbies
some have stated I'm violent at a price
my life though is mine spending time
knowing I'm with my product
without guilt or sorrow
Can the next man say that?
with an agitator right in his eyes
maybe, maybe not
yeah...
I met my oneness
and greeted it this time around
what remains in my mind
as significant about the episode is that
unlike a couple of years ago
this time...

My oneness gave me the right of way

ONE TRACK AT A MIND

It's not easy to one track a mind purposely
holding so many small ideas
that a single line is what's needed
to keep everyday life's thoughts flowing efficiently
stepping off the ride of majority for sanity
slow how it goes...

how life keeps a found structure when you brace it properly
there's no need to be schizoid hectic
walking...
two step
double time in a normal paced lane
when you don't have to be
it takes a minute in a fast-paced world
to figure that out
lower the stress for self no doubt

coffee
caffeine and diamond lanes
with drum and bass popping through the eardrums
don't swerve if it ain't necessary
chill even if you have or have not had your capacity fill

one smooth focus of attention span
in actual life, while the world spins
to make good on the blessings promised
one of them is the term described as CALM

I've learned how to stack a house
heavier by the ounce
it'll be good for the complex mind
to stay in step by step line
with one topic from beginning to end

Who knows how the rest might fade?
but fade they all eventually do
the key is...
In the end of your journey,
Did you gain...?
or end up in a rumpled mess...

Thoughts on one tracking the mind
amongst a bunch of tangled ideas and topics

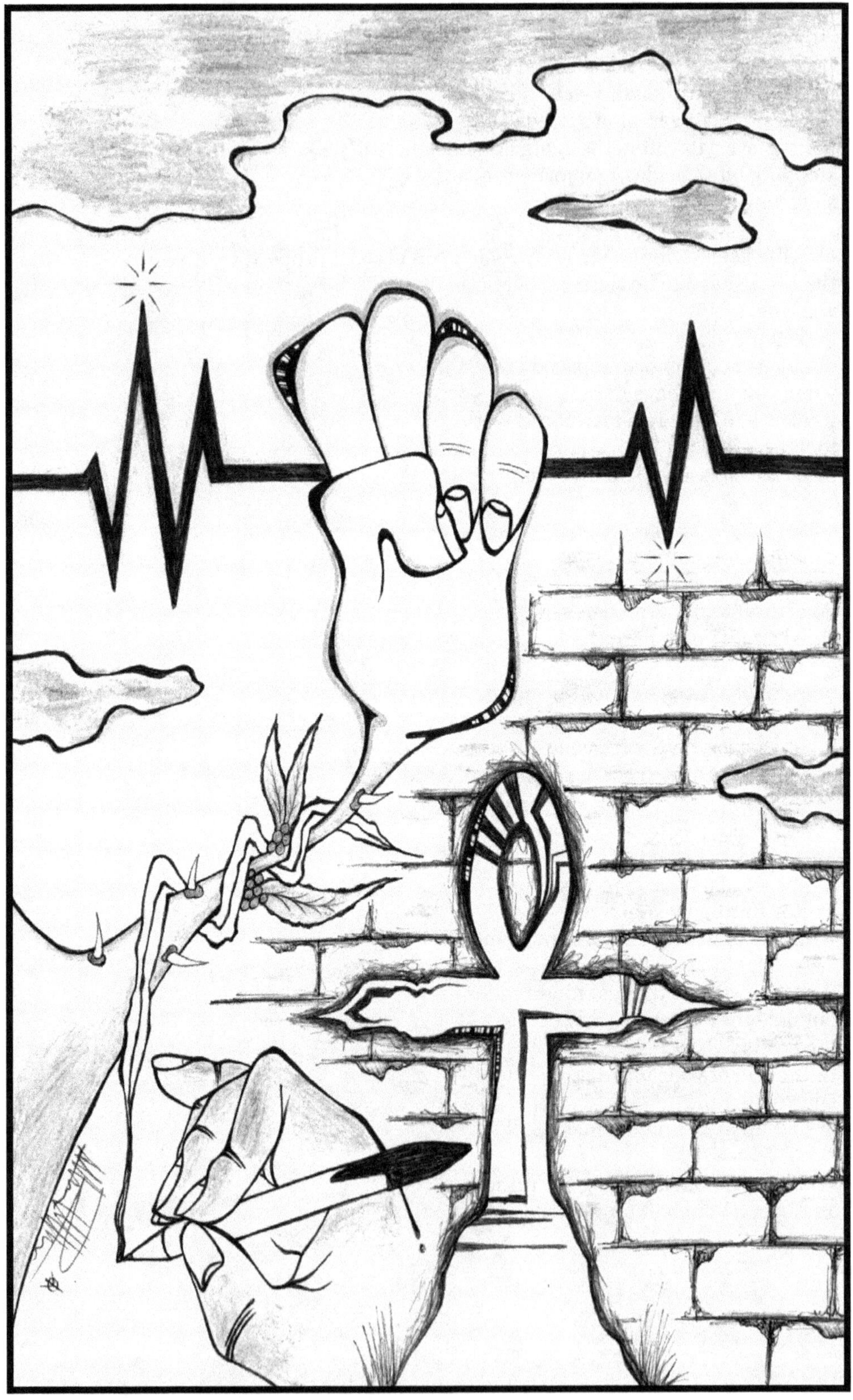

ODE TO POETRY

In trust of not disgust
I hope you can receive this
flow of words floating off of me
with undisclosed direction
magically with a level of discretion, ohhh...
how the soul needs to be stroked at times
in configuration of caress
as you vibe to this reading
words coming together just to strum
the melodic overtone of life
that is signified by expression
humbly as all goes
sound chimes ringing through earholes
letters set to eyesight for purpose
that is poetry...

There is so much some can choose to say as connection
sometimes there is nothing
dignified as right in just absorb
the world is bigger than our finite imagination
so much to intake and reflect
and poetry is a reflection with a rhythm to it
for the receiver of the gift given to follow along to
if he can catch it
all within art
trusting to the realm of artists
who are creating it

Poetry
phrases of distinction to leave an impression
of the scenery or more it describes
brought forth by means of arrangement
meant to evoke emotions
in that it might have a message
other times simply put together
for the sake of finesse
language at its elegant hour
some might never sour
from the interaction with commune...
-ication tools adjusted for their palette
so much that has been placed
as an addition to lives in an infinite standing

That is poetry

TANGENT

I write sometimes to express thought
I write sometimes in a break from everyday things
hopefully writing can ease the tension
and apprehension within a worldly outlook
and adjusting to a bunch of new environments placed into
that the reader can't fully grasp
with hope they won't ever have to hold the cup
of a man going through divorce and incarceration
with no finish to his education
all let known in a singsong fashion
maybe as such the reader may only notice
if the reader is just self
sometimes these writings are a just a break off of monotony
for self...
overly entranced with self
Does that matter?
needing nothing at all if he, or she isn't listening
so I went off on a tangent

Thoughts in a broken chain
shall be burnt to ashes
if they are reborn as a beautiful phoenix
it's beauty was not due to I...

Please take note to that and let me know
if my words start to attack
in a backlash of not being attention getters
on a tangent
I'm off on it again...

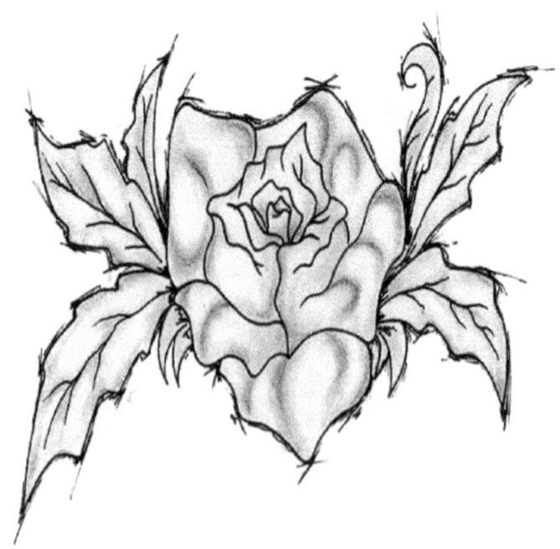

GOES FOR NOW

There's no flow for cell walls and doors
looking at life through a release date hour glass
I'm counting my time slowly trying to scheme on speed
plans in place for a changed something
whatever that means, and whatever that brings
staying away from dayroom drama
soap opera in shackles and prison blues
can't be for me
mind focused on freedom, as it should be
making my moves and marinating best ways possible
old school music in my ears
to keep my attitude cool
I'm making myself calm
collect
the reeducation process understands that
never mind street life time I missed
working criminal thinking errors out
so I can readjust
trust the double take on plays and moves made
just building me more now as a rock
solid house with goals accomplished
how it should be
don't counteract to that
that's the downplay I'm watching for in response
so I can deal with it more properly
meditation in handcuffs
allowing this reflect of teach
my first steps back to the streets
are to show the radiance of my release
rhythmic
a little bit more rhythmic now
as my freedom stride regains a casual stroll
blessed with soul
carried away for a time of reminisce
of the actual city I missed
I'm eventually to greet it with a kiss
a new early morning each day
to relax and do this
slow...
it goes for now

UNTITLED

KNOW WHO YOU IZ...
you need to know where you coming from
remember that
cold attitude cocked as I...
fire spark for education
purpose for the teach
waking them up son...

from the battlegrounds to the...
edge of your speak
watch your think
as my mind remains clear of intoxicants
and the strains of altered irritants
blessed with a cleansing
where it was needed

Can you cope with your high
if I'm soberly at you, kid?

Let the truth of life tell its side to this
no need for mic-time
if I'm loud speaking well through a bullhorn
warned motions of a soul courted
repeatedly with extra drama to handle,
scandalous...

Making my finesse moves well
I know my final destination and how to get there
cats cross paths and face railroad hits
as I'm on coast like you ain't seen nothing
go back and clutch tight to your education goals
orientation from here...
I'm head of class in a steady release of emotion

How's that manifest?
come get greeted with the means
write myself into a groove with thoughts patch worked
to create a Frankenstein monster for your ears
and/or eyes to trace the stitches of connected parts...

Thus...
it's the project for the day

LOVELY LADY

Lovely lady
Can I come satisfy you slowly?
I'm here now so...
grace be to the way you got me
I'm to your side
let me thoroughly greet you
with what you were wishing for
without missing a beat or a step
womanly elegance
enuff to keep me entranced all evening
you've been protective of your feelings
I hope you have no problem
with being open with me alone
How do you truly feel?
What's on your precious mind?
Can I say something sweet to set it off?
make you smile a bit...
with a little more depth
than a sweet nothing sista
your time shouldn't
and will not be wasted
stay in tune with me and the lovemaking
of minds in connection
that feeds the physical stimulation
intertwining auras...
there's so much stress in this world
please relax with a lyrical
spiritual backrub by candlelight
Can you handle it?
don't be vexed by the lane I'm giving
hopefully foreshadowing
an intense romantic evening
with this poem as foreplay
listening to music
as a sweet ballad backdrop
for a mystical side combined with us

Lovely lady
Can I come satisfy you slowly?
grace be to the way you got me...

SO FINE

Her body marches through my eyes
leaving me at attention
hopelessly
the grace of her beauty
is enuff for a forest fire
got my manhood damningly
high strung level tense
I haven't seen a woman who could do that
for quite a while
strutting her stuff
you go girl...
strutting your stuff
thick
sexy
smooth
leaving me nothing to guess at
with that outfit
right...
extra small
extra tight
the grip it hugs you with
makes me jealous of it
you hurting the whole game
I know it
body solid where it's good
a brick house
ain't the word for the lusciousness
you were womanly blessed with
let me pause...
just to get a grip
oh, the delight to be hugging those hips
would make an older man's heart skip
to be near you
must be just a step away from heaven
I haven't seen a lady
so lavishly dashing
in my recent recollection
setting off wind chimes
in my sexual senses
but alas...
with all that expressed
she didn't even give me the damn digits

I GLIDE AWAY

And with the grace of an eagle
I glide away from my incarcerated mind state

Yard locked for something or other
my time rolling by
like trying to melt frozen rubber
dragging along at two miles per hour
my soul surviving in the beast
devoured by the machine
someday I'll gain my life back
for now, it's forward march
for this alley cat candidly reflecting
on a life held at bay
more importantly
more potent with each spent day
rebuilding a situation of broken clay
is my homecoming
handling a battled hold of self
walking out of darkness continually
bless the blind faith from within
sometimes now the cell walls
speak to me
I answer back
when I snatch a solitary moment of chance

And with the grace of an eagle
I glide away from my incarcerated mind state

As a new day begins at 5:30 AM
looking forward to my state pay
as my state blues slowly fade
as time passes
I find less and less to say
quietly keep my temper from roasting
playing host to the sanctions
imposed on my square
and from my cipher of self
hopefully a positive energy conveyed
from where I've been
and what I'm on
I used to be a ticking time bomb
but now I can hit the streets
noticeably different in presentation
the same as the seasons change
I'm holding face cards
as far as game
I've made many mistakes before though

witness to the way
my life and times were rearranged
systematic control
mental health paying its way
I found out there was a toll
as long as it's not breaking spiritual goals
waiting for my style of society
I've once called home
that which I've once known

And with the grace of an eagle
I glide away from my incarcerated mind state

I spend an ample amount of time in flight
to Destination X
unknown to overseers
eager at the chance to break the shackles
that held me for so long
dusting off years stored away
I've pulled my motion forward
toward a new horizon
with no chains or pepper spray
bless the holding force of freedom
as I glide...
as I fly...

And with the grace of an eagle
I glide away from my incarcerated mind state

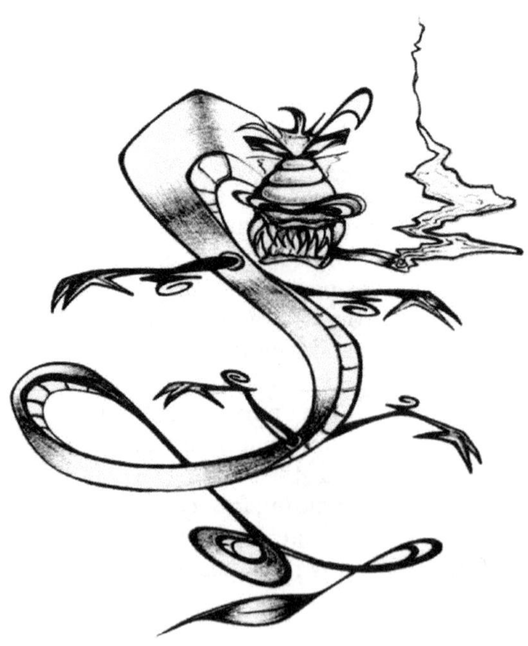

SO IT GOES, BOTH HANDS ON YOUR SOUL

So you want test
I'm an end to the drama
keep it complex
and I'm a lid flipper
with a much calmer flow
than it's ever been
no concern whether you breathe again
my style walks like a Doberman
pinch
to the point of pain
in my pleasure stroke
you can go for broke
and still can't cope
with the way I lay tracks
I'm solid
no games
my thoughts the same
as it's ever been
me giving up on rhyme
that's a mortal sin
combined with matter of fact
blessed black spirit
my ism indiscreetly meets your mind
like the shot of a cannonball blast
greet you like your adjustment
to my approach was makeshift
how's that to speak of steez
please be wary, forewarned
so it goes
both hands on your soul
as I roll...
spark...
and smoke your attention
attentively

Come correct in brick fashion
words get plastered to the ceiling in my realm
I took the helm as captain a long time ago
holding firm
the wayward souls
with free writing
freethinking commands attention
even in misgivings
how's it put to use?
as it shifts with breeze
for thoughts...
motivated in print if you like to read

braille if you can't see
and tinted hot sauce if you like it spicy
split the darkness like a locker box hit
to the head kid...
so it goes
both hands on your soul
as I roll...
spark...
and smoke your attention
attentively

The way words take a wayward spin
is as easy as bad karma
not to downgrade
but to make sure you know
not to take words lightly
as eventually
we're all to become
dust in the wind
from the nuclear age of terminology
a nuclear physicist could have figured it
I'm giving it
to, to, to you
after it came to me
after one hit
I didn't inhale it
presented again to me gently
so it goes
both hands on your soul
as I roll...
spark...
and smoke your attention
attentively

BLESS THE TENDERNESS

Diligently and slowly
stroke the sublime part of your mind
with my intention to instill
caressed word twist of a sexually arousing nature
the way the words play host to stimulus signature
description of the encrypted messaging
being transmitted rhythmically
over flow for the sake of loving
what it's worth physically
touching you in the right spot
after knit-picking for the comfort zone
can be a task or undertaking
I might never oppose
holding you softly
like a blooming rose or lotus
letting me know it's us
that togetherness is just
and to speak of love is a must
emotions holding
not repressed but refined
in the openness that is everyday life refined
sanctified to the art of intertwined growth
I hope the feeling is one that is mutual
something I should already know
my hold to you in this world
should never grow old or fade
Dare I let it loosen up?
oh, how to let an entity know
that they are truly godsend
I'm ready to make you feel rapture delight
in every step if I'm kept
and God forbid
my being overbearing or over obsessive
sometimes your flowering soul
leaves me overwhelmed
delicate soul
bless the tenderness
I'm yours for the taking

Bless the tenderness
I'm yours for the taking

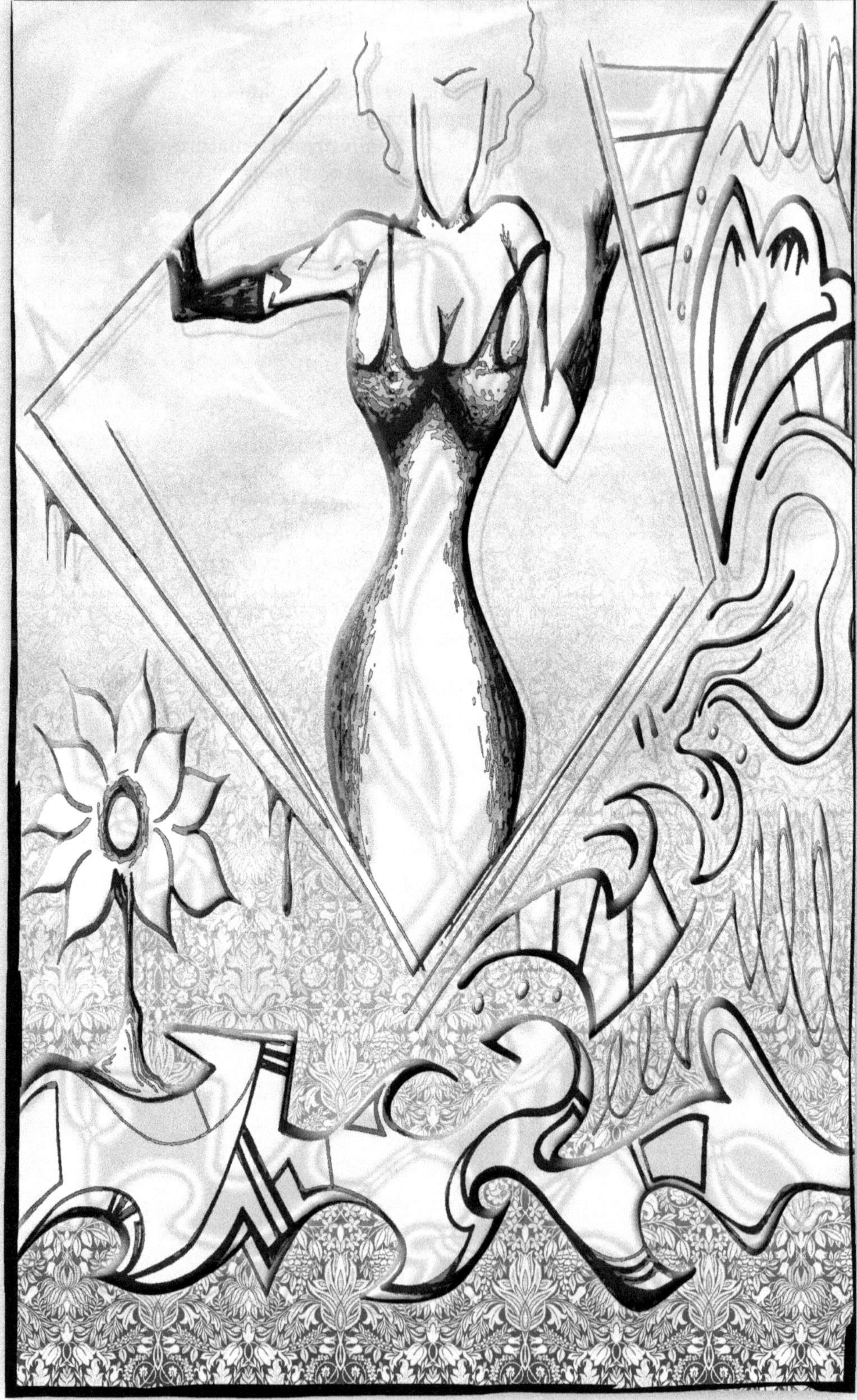

WAITING

Her silhouette showed no age
just grace in its voluptuousness
the type of beauty to hold
her curves definitely an hourglass
imprint in my mind timeless
she can make a man hot like fire
with her presence
a man can have a mentally fulfilling climax
with the thoughts of her sweetness
dew dripping making a man
long for her taste
just a sip
tingling in the imagination of her body wet
even her sweat breathes
all that a woman should be
Can I remain brave and ask her name?
I've seen her so many times before
it's not so farfetched to think
and believe she made me obsessed
she may or may not have been
a treasure to be possessed though
as beauty and lust are just cuts
and grooves so far deep
Does she even have time to cater to it?
As a matter of fact, do I?
reasons for passing glances
racing thoughts in non-speak
the something that becomes a problem
if unaddressed for too long
that's how much yearn
the slight burn...
is desire to become interlocked
in life and spirit
the cool...
is the continued calm of the whole situation
inner beauty shines even in silence
sometimes she's golden hued
a sign as much as anything
wondering if she can see my tint
Is it comforting?
one day she might come out of a shell of her own
and approach me
until then though
I'm just waiting

MIND DOODLING

Cool, calm collect
as words
make it all sooth like ice
next time around
recognized as that nice
as ink spills the pages
my mind tracks the next step
in an organized fashion
come to terms
with correct effervescence
in flight
float eventfully through
the side of neck
in height unimaginable

Mind doodling
the vivid creativeness
has its own grip of the paper
leaving trails of lettering to follow

COME FOLLOW ME

Abstract deluxe is the trip
the hop and skip
are the motions to master
methods to grab ya
respond becuz
it has been snatching and biting ‘atcha
placed as emotionlessly and carelessly
as radio gaga
What do you need to add to a mind doodle?

I can easily free my mind
and consume my time
by scribbling and chicken scratching on yours
Would it be a bother?

Not to jeopardize anything...

Just to get some funky off
How would that be and stand?
after I allow you to regain the reigns
conceptual poetic, without a concept
having no purpose but time kill
might be overkill

How do you choose to believe it?
a mind doodle
free hand onto the mental subject
in objectiveness remains to be
named and focused on

Hey there!
gal and guy
letting thoughts linger unaddressed
I hope this moment wasted
wasn't completely a bore
if it was un-educational
as another hair on the head fades to white
in the general age of
momentous awakening

Mind doodling
ready for the story to begin

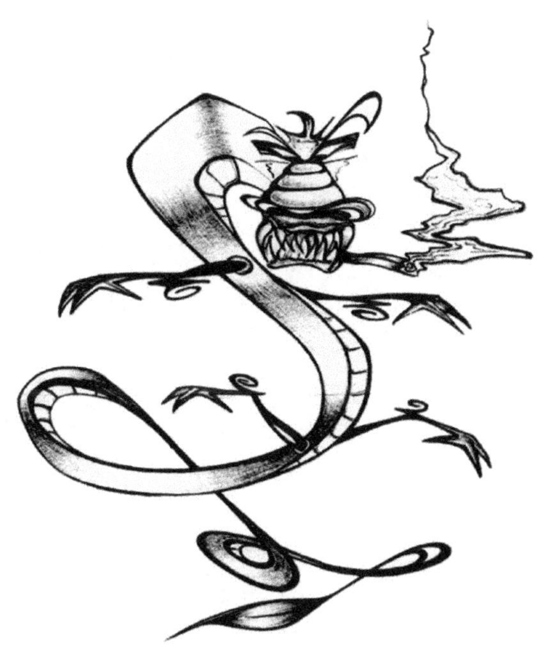

MEMORIES

Chasing time wasted away
hopes to grab something enlightening
memories are all that keep past life precious
immaterial essence of what was once accomplished
and held sacred
as thoughts of achievement
and the reach for it
occupy past remembrances
the distant tomorrow
is a new challenge
soon to become a past memory

UNTITLED

You and I had pleasant times together
I managed to ruin the love we built
with my transgressions
making a new day is something
I must learn now and make it manage
adjusting to another's emotional scars
is something that I must deal with
especially if I'm the cause for the drama
a way to fix it
Can it come by me?

B-A-D

BAD karma coupled with BAD luck
Brought chains and divorce
BAD attitude and BAD outlook
Made times much worse
BAD direction and BAD timing
Has too much energy focused on the wrong outcomes
BORN AND DIED
Shouldn't be the best thing they say about my accomplishments
BORN AND DIED
Hopefully not my ultimate description

Now...
BELIEVED AND DID
could be made to fit properly
with a positive adjustment
BROKE AND DUMB
holds no boundary as to how negative
bad, bad, decisions
with bad insight
never can fit me comfortably
So now, how about a change?
when the old me is dead and gone...
How much of the bad will be buried with it?

MATTER OF MENTION

I thought the time given would help cultivate me as a writer
topic matter has left such a blank
I feel sometimes that I've been clean scraped with bleach
time to grow is what has manifested
with the world at a distance I can't deny
there is a somewhat lack of tension
ease of apprehension
towards the outside world and odds that led to containment
make the best of the nature of the state of my containment
while others laugh it all off
I'm steady thinking
awake wide
in reality living not just a melancholy dream
weaving hopes for a quicker tomorrow are now the mental occupation
as the growth process is slow like basking in a never-ending sunset
if I were more optimistic I'd have said sunrise
at times I rise facing another step to the mountain slowing me down
just to move forward again
another gain
still images unlocked
away from failure stains
at times in life the momentum quickening the stride
easing the tension
kicking up dust
wind driven
spirit gliding across the fertile matter of topic that was once nothingness
now being visualized into something to be read and mentioned on
freedom flowing
it was washed clean and more pure in the blank space
that it was discovered in just moments before
freedom flowing is what becomes of the matter of mention
discovering a matter of mention

EARTHLY ANGEL

An earthly angel is what I realized
I never took the time to address her as such
so much help given
How could her efforts have been overlooked?
my eyes blind to the real for years
after so many mistakes I've made
will I get another chance with an earthly angel?
though I missed her shine as an inner city goddess
blessed with a positive aura
as the world continued to get more negative
around and surrounding
her actions still stayed focused
her helpful attitude wasn't realized by me
until it was too late to make amends for mistakes
lack of judgment in a proper prospective ran her away
I know now by the solitude I'm left lingering with
without her now my nights are cold
none of her warmth even in simple gestures
to comfort my presence
she was truly something wonderful
it's a shame that I'm too late to realize it
she even warned of it
my heart left broken after I broke hers
concerning her dreams of a companionship with me
I suppose hurting an earthly angel
event still unpardonable
is a part of me

EXPRESSIONAL OUTLET

Expressional outlet
others can stay stuck not knowing the how and why
why and how
understanding for self is the most important sweat from my brow
others get vexed looking for factors of dominance
not finding it in the creative variance living from within
expressional outlet

In need of that energy output
with thoughts ready to ambush
making over whatever non-action
getting plowed as expressions burst out
whether outdated out of place in an attitude
fitting the situation
sometimes not...
half cooked sometimes simmering
for a night's stand placed with timing
and an able hand
expressions in outlet

Voice to microphone
pen to pad un-caged
unleashed
each continued fill to the blanks
is not as much a trail
as it is a tail to the travelling
taking place like a comet's ass o' funk
following the orbit to the continued thought complex
around the make of the individual
the divided usual needing some way of release
could be stricken by happiness or grief
waiting for ways to let the inner feeling be known
sometimes shown through expressions that are outward

Electricity set forth that is our expressional outlet

MEDITATED

I THOUGHT I WAS DEEP

I was going over my usual
the humdrum of my inner skull
the motion that fills the inner region
then I realized I have no seasoning
if any...
then maybe not enuff
How could I have made it all this time?
overcooked and stuffed
without the flavor for the average palette
maybe I should be more humorous or morbid
How to make the most of my bland situation?
as shallow as it seems
I thought I was deep...

CLIMAX

Fiendin' for your G-spot
not doubting
Imma get it
magnificent when I hit it
us vibing in an unmatched harmony
I've become one with our stroking motion
intense...
taking you to your ecstasy
you say, "Come hard for me"
like you owe it to me girl
I want you to feel the effervescence
it's the relaxation to the stroke
you've been waiting on
warm inside slightly cooked on the outer
making you moan upon my arrival in touch

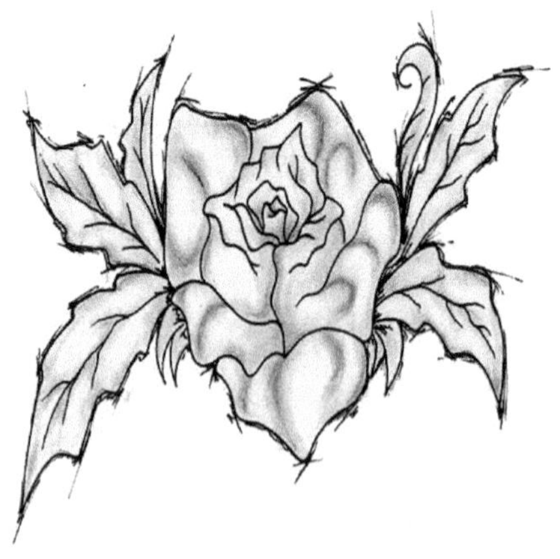

COMPLEX

Seeking life
I found myself double-teamed by death on both sides
calling my name
I begin to get filled with anxiety
perplexed complex
Can I make it out of this mess?
sunlight saves this void of a man that I am
yet, I'm totally engulfed in darkness
hypocrite
haven't flexed enuff pull in life
not enuff show of grit
solutions to problems slip away
with every day I vacate
instead of staying to work it out

Filled with anxiety
perplexed complex
Can I make it out of this mess?
with no lifejacket
still mad I never had it
sinking in my debt
my wage of sin, death
but the dark side can't have it
still I'm anxious to rid the dilemma from the world
faithfully, I'm to my fate

So dear love...
don't be so strung over my path
en route to my next destination
in high definition
making sure the world has swung its attention
to the complications of a sinner
ever wound down into the cavern of distress
there you have it
my one and only true confession
for the mayhem that I stepped up and made
trying to find my way out of myself as a lesser man
perplexed by a self-inflicted complex
knowing what a mess I done made

TAKE HOLD

The highlight of life now
writing about it
sure to grab focus
making a topic matter
I put the earth on simmer
to let the ice of "avoiding a point" melt
here I am again
trying to find something to say
trying to be as easygoing as a breeze's sway
trying to make it another day
trying to be a writer that mattered
high-strung son of a gun
label my words as loaded with bullets
to leave a whole plane of existence
changed by the words I cultivate
in demonstrate of the effort taken
justified in the deliverance of a message
whether it's initially realized or not
positioned lukewarm
for the right mix of go-getter and reluctant-ness
if that formula can be fitting a walk through poetry
with a whole heart of more to say and do
don't be a fool who thought wrong
about the mission statement
but I'm still writing
man I'm...
holding onto a glimmer of that zone
trying to stay put in levitate
with words in swing for a ride
so the receiver can enjoy and take hold

DERELICT TO SOCIETY

If I wrote every day
Would it make a difference to the powers that be?
people incarcerated for mistakes as far as the eye can see
Am I glad to be a citizen of this country?
knowing we need change
hanging on to the hope for revolution
understanding that after a conviction it starts with self
so I have to make my mentality ready for it

Put the drugs away partner

So I can pay attention to freedom coming my way
without another prison number or welfare line
or maybe that's just the psyche medication talking
hoping my last breath isn't attached to a crack pipe

Who keeps stealing my lifeline?!

Can I get a side of hot sauce with that black president ordered in
or is this just an attempt at forgiveness for the slave trade?
made in exasperation
Who is true to some politicking instead of the ***poliTRICKS*** played?
anyways, I still got to make it off the street
before you can see me intellectually debating
our present situation
so as we hold hands and sing
remember we shall overcome the abortion clinics and hopefully
the liquor store on every corner
giving my last five American dollars to foreigners nightly
as the police passing by truly view me as a derelict to society

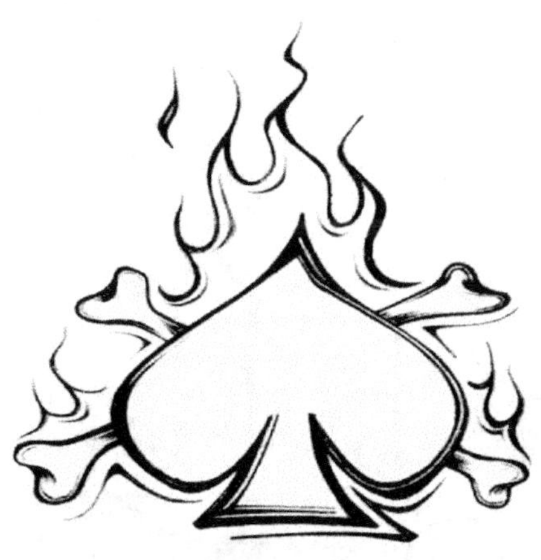

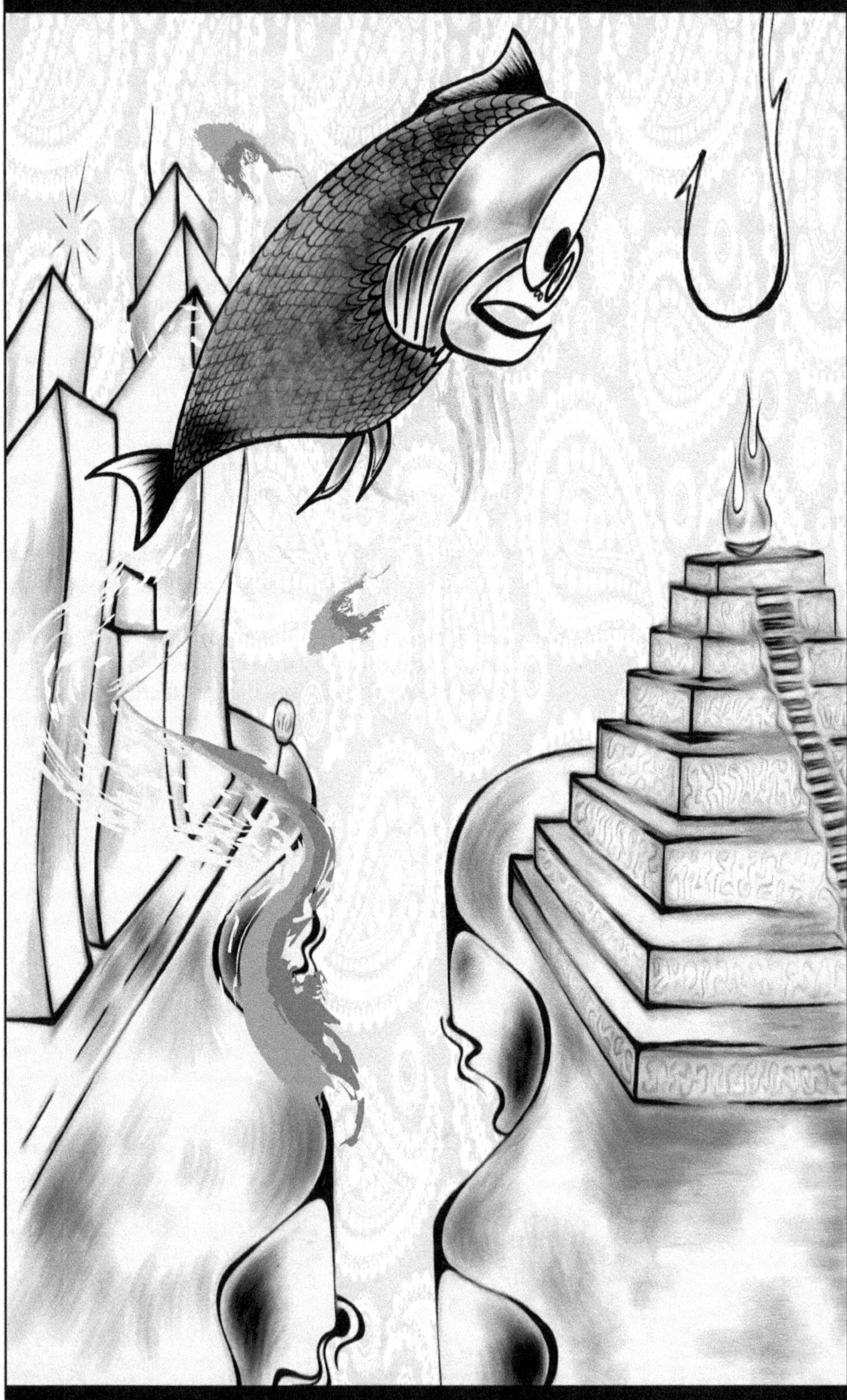

TORMENT OF FREETHINK

I had a flash of Omni-potency
but it wore off
I was the big fish in a little pond
but only in my head
my surroundings were too grand
for my anti-social being
limited to the relaxed state of reclusiveness
happy to be trapped in seclusion
with a notepad
just so, I can document my whole episode
as I cook and toast my memory for factual detail
I replay my existence instantly
at a snail's pace
so I can be over-compulsive about
being about something
with the attention span of a flea
in a large empty room, of course
I don't want to hurt nothing...
Who can beside somebody who is beside themselves?
there ain't no standing room
and I'm still in awe of my manic state of doom
when I was a little chicken
scared that the world collapsed
hypothetically speaking
sinking in my want for everlasting tranquility
unable to stop the ripples in the lake
becuz of my pouting and splashing
suffocating myself
in my own TORMENT OF FREETHINK

FOCUS

A physician wants me to understand my mental illness...

My only condition needed to be up for informed discussion
isn't denial...

Only the whys for my trials and tribulations
I'm too overly disorderly as a being
to state that I simply have a disorder of the brain
branded by chemical imbalance
hopefully alcohol can be an equalizer
until I learned, it was a contributing factor to faults
as I spend precious time walking a fault line socially
and losing touch more and more with healthy culture
not knowing if I can endure more anxiety
being violent at times
I'm victimizing family surrounding
with less regard to surrounding population
like the repercussions won't come back to me
creating a lifelong mess...

What have I become?
affected inside schizophrenia
maybe if I play it close and tell the physician
what he needs to know
I can prevent more traumas
and even Pinocchio nose growth
I lost my humor along the way
so please bear with me
possible all caused by genetic abnormality or other factors
leaving me extreme in my mood swing
fighting hallucinations
what it's like in this position
leading to another panic attack
confused
delusional
until I realized I needed to have more focus...

SHE'S BEAUTIFUL

I can focus on the way your body sways when you walk
I can pay the high cost of attention all day
as a matter of fact sunshine
you make my day when you walk in the room
you light it up
electricity from the grace of continuous movement
maybe I'll ask to take you dancing
when my hormones calm down a little bit
entranced still with your aura

ETERNITY

I started my day uptight
until I thought about the happiness I had
when I was with you
so I reminisced all day of better times together
hopefully when we meet again it will be
never to depart from one another
our next time shared should be for an eternity

TRAPPED WITHIN IT

Distressed by captivity captivating
I'm behind concertina wire and fences
walls and bricks
becuz society is supposed to have a fear of me
Was my position as a prisoner that great of a feat
for the state to accomplish?

While I'm here...
How about a program or two slated for my rehabilitation?
becuz all I've seen so far...
is a table for spades and chin-up bars
elders walking by with a look like...
cheer up young buck
you might still have a life pending release
if everything didn't vanish the moment my guilty verdict came

What's out there for me to be kept away from?
coping with the thoughts and ideas
of penitentiary life setting in
I'm learning to be my own best friend
keeping a watchful eye to the jive-shuckers around me
scheming for another shot of coffee
to make the day go past
floating faces in the midst looking aged and sad
not so much dazed and confused from the follies of youth
getting paid for with time chiseled off of life
that could be lived more productive
doing anything besides wasting away in a cell
got herds of individuals salivating at the chance
to taste freedom's chill air once again
only escape being the nightly dreams
and nightly news when a person can relate
to the events described on TV screens

Spending much precious on drowning away in current events
hoping to stay in touch with the outside world
best ways possible
until the chow is served again

Not sure of the time of day
just sure that for now
I'm forced here to stay
so let me keep my distance from the C.O.'s
looking to hole shot somebody
making all this a little unbearable
dealing with a desperate system that got me trapped within it

TRAPPED

My mind becoming jelly
in the flux of matter, that was stress
I didn't have an escape from the sweat
coming from my fresh new drama filled head
worried about all the misgivings
and non-repented deeds
nothing I could walk away from
trapped, I was trapped

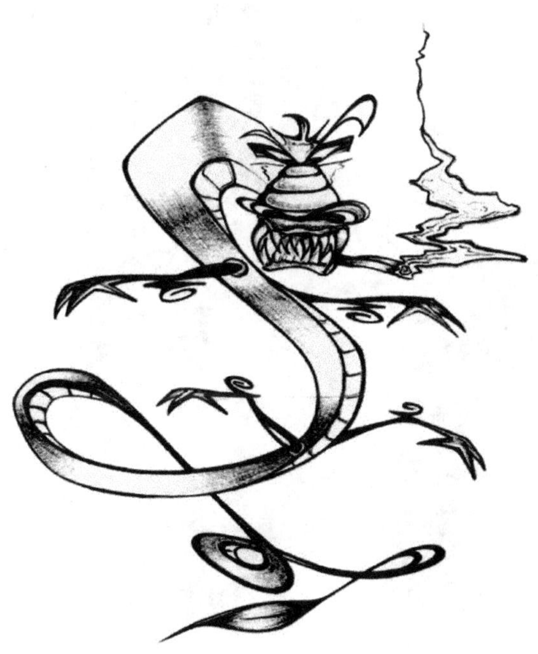

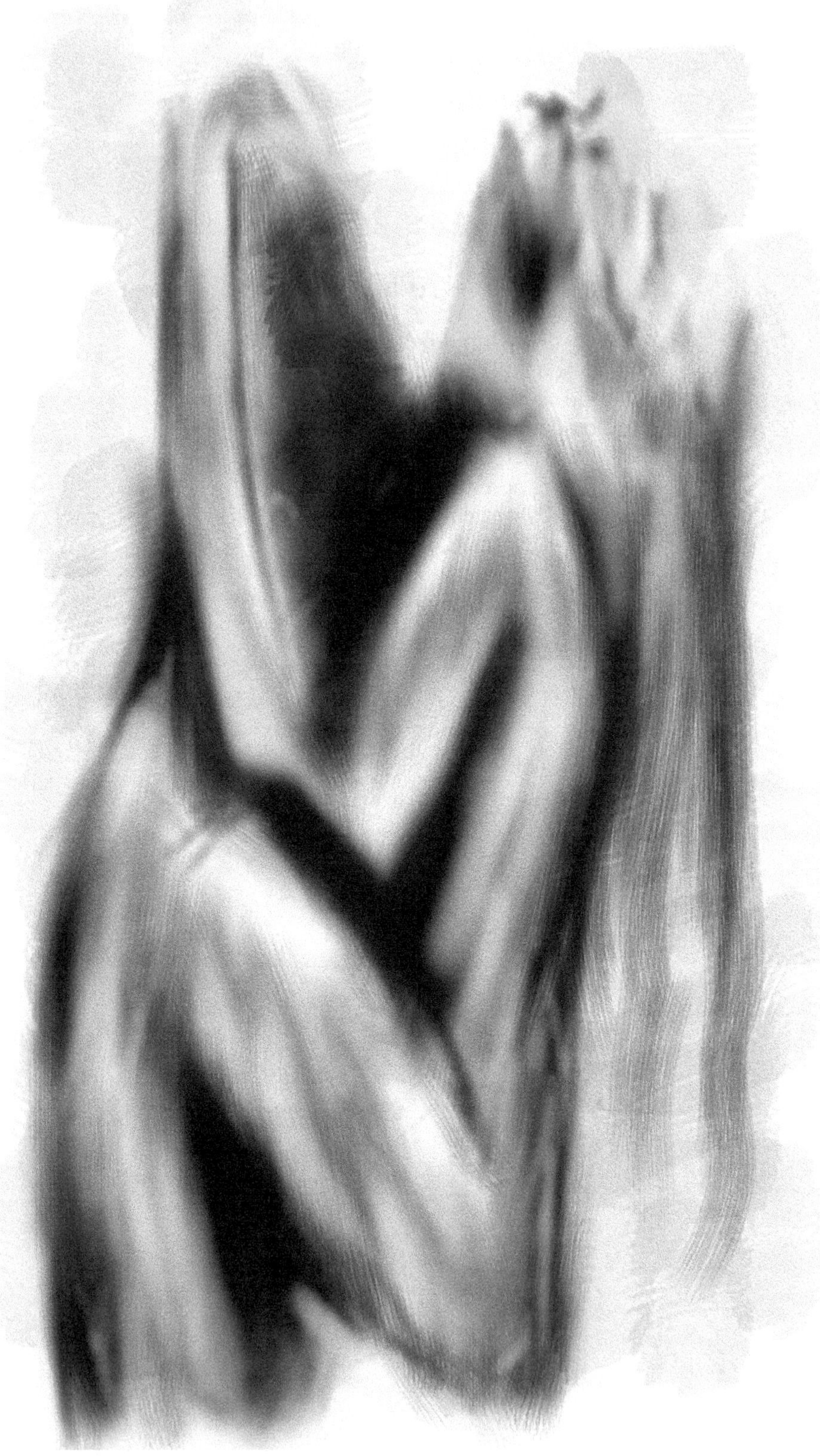

HOLDING ME TIGHT

Slow wined in twilight
your body has a beautiful aura holding me tight

Lovemaking motion that's as gentle as an ocean mist breeze
soothing to our private scenery
closed door
closed set
for the two of us
interlocked trust between our connect
expressed in the embrace of our eyes
in contact sensually
feelings of enchantment
the emotion set free

Slow wined in twilight
your body has a beautiful aura holding me tight

We share something special
every time we build
love bug pricked us with a quill on purpose
Why it chose us?
it's shown in our moonlight dance
jonesin' for a closer bond
being with you is something to be terribly fond of
the time we share is as pure as the thoughts of doves and lace
keeping us naturally high at a gentle pace

Slow wined in twilight
your body has a beautiful aura holding me tight

I move slow, so I don't rush this motion
coast easily to a comfortable state
oneness is a definite description of our connect
I know that as we intertwine
our bond becomes more and more complex
every climax is a treasured experience
with you is where my heart is

STENCH OF CONTAINMENT

Entangled in the stench of containment
exhausted and spent
grinding and hoping for a revolution
that don't look like its coming
I had faith in myself not to trust a system
that rejected me
now I feel myself slowly conceding
to the workings that detained me until...

I woke up and that mundane of despair
struck and touched
I felt again disgust for my current situation
so I keep myself enlightened
to a better outcome inside a change
that was professed before my time
it's a long mile coming and going
understanding my trappings holding me

They are a political, social dooming
with more negative looming
being graced when I slip
can't cope or grip ideas of violence
and the thought of being a product perpetuating
it's how the holding system saves face
at that...

Bloodsucking money for the cause
waiting for the next man's fall
off to the races and place your bet
on the one who is first to the slave ships
with big brother watching
from the captain's seat

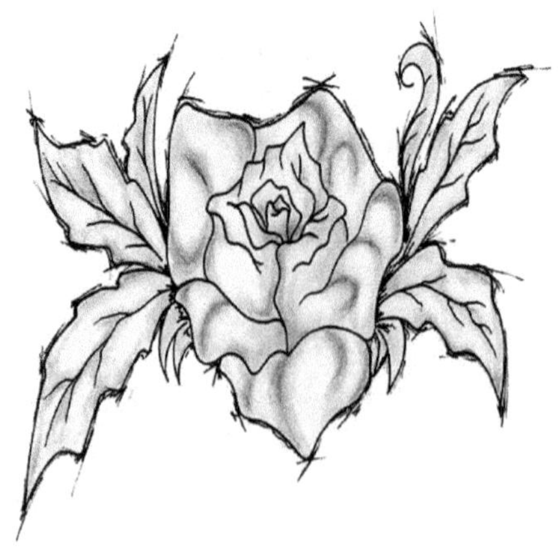

WITH A NEW PEN

I suspect...

With a new pen I can start
or start over again
something I put in motion
and document holdings
of vast amount of feelings
placed in empty space
filling empty pages upon pages
in front of my presence
Would it matter much?
the lives I could touch
with expression

TIRED OF LIFE'S GAMES

I guess the ledge might be known for it's reach
but I'm yet a step away from death and defeat
the thought of overcoming it might be
where I'm basking in defeat
Would I be dead to the world and a failure?
if I tell ya that I know the ledge
after the bad and terrible predicaments I've been in
frustrated hoping for a way to adjust to the terrain
tired of life's games

YOU SHOULD BE SOOTHED

Attitude and body rhythm
elegant
your air has no arrogance
just soulful taste and tact
a wonderful woman you must be
simply beauty
I wish I could ask you to be with me
Can you believe in me?
I hope I don't disrupt your groove

If I could
I would put a rose petal down
for your every move
harmony is one with you
and I could tell
maybe it's in the cultured grace
showing you're silk and smooth
you should be soothed

FREE THE THOUGHT

Scribbling out thoughts I don't want
and keeping close to those that please
ease of thought
claiming territory with every letter
phrases held together by the grip of ideas
Ideals ripping across to the receiver
of the rhyme and the style
while all is perceived and accounted for indirectly

Slides through odysseys of words and stanzas
become the mode of travel
theatrical
it's magical how much is shared
with or without a guilt trip
holding nothing back
so used to it
these writings take on a life they already own
waiting for the deed bought and paid for
don't ask about the legitimacy
intimately and ultimately
the victors of their own freedom...

I release them
I'm still the tyrant until I do
the overseer
landlord
bored and uptight
with much on my mind
that needs to be weaned from me
so be patient if your heart skips at all
with my crack of the whip

WHAT MOOD SHOULD I WEAR TODAY?

I woke up in good spirits
took to my rituals without having a nervous fit
as the sun shines
I know I'm blessed kinetic
But what mood should I wear today?

Yesterday was hectic
sort of like a bother
I ended up bored in my daily duty of chores
so my emotions reflected all of it
But what mood should I wear today?

Every day can't be marvelous
sometimes the time is more than vicious enuff
to make a man depressed
making moves knowing there are repercussions
some days are downtrodden with a dead end
for an end point
should be a vanishing point
joined with more bad news
of bullet ridden homes and schools at that
now we have to duck terrorists
But what mood should I wear today?

If I could be happy all the while
I would go the extra mile to smile
but sometimes life at hand
doesn't call for it
Should I ruin another's sway?
just making another step away
with the dismay that I project
not protected from the bipolar swing
I might be capable of
I'm no dove
especially if the mood I chose was a bad one
cross me wrong
and you might just catch it bad son
the mood that suits me shouldn't reflect
the violence of our era though
so I stay a firm believer in benevolence
even if my energy is spent
becuz I can't justify a foul attitude

GOD BLESS YOUR SOUL

There is so much I want to say to you
excuse me if I'm not as singsong rhythmic when I project
remember with love...
patience...
as I pause...
I take another breath of life
I should be spending with you
I could breathe easier if
I knew we would stay together forever
and forever might not last as long as my love for you
know that it is true
that I couldn't stand to lose you
or be without you
there's no limit to what I want to express
but I'm at a loss for words
stunned...
frozen at times by the thoughts I have
and how to share them
you captivate me
when you captivate my mind
the world around me stops on a thin dime
and as the earth stands still
I know the love I have is real
and you make me want to share it with you

God bless your soul

HOLDING YOU

If I was holding you
you wouldn't have to face loneliness
I'd be the companion by your side

If I was holding you
you wouldn't need to fear the darkness
I'd make sure your path was lit

If I was holding you
everything would be all right
there wouldn't be that feeling of despair or desperation
my hands would generate loving, kind warmth to keep you

If I was holding you
I would keep you as tranquil as possible
so you can finally manage to be at ease in peace

If I was holding you
I would be the comforter that you were hoping for
when your tears were flowing

If I was holding you
I would be there with a bit of sunshine
to keep your eyes dry when you think of crying
and make sure you never have to return
to that state of sadness again

If I was holding you
I'd make sure to treat you gently
with the respect that your soul has been longing for
If I was holding you...

Come close...
so I can just hold you

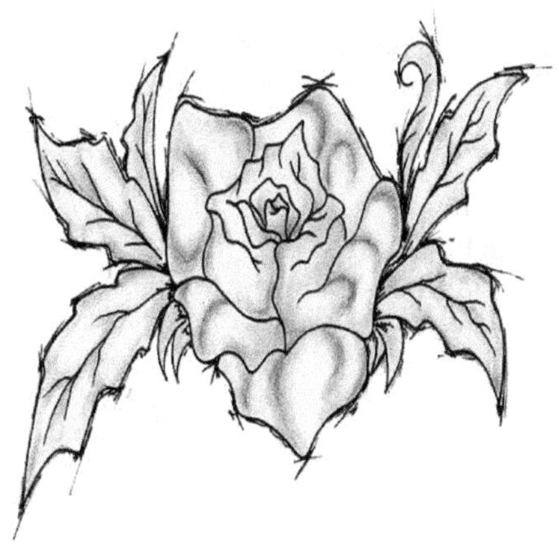

FOR SOMEONE CLOSE

It's a strange day
I can't think of nothing to say
to someone who should be up close
yet they are so far away
Imagine what time does to distance
I didn't try to get distant
you used to be distinct to me
now fading as a face in passing

For friendship's sake
I hope there is still pull and reach
to bridge a gap in between us
It might not be me you trust
but spite and disgust isn't necessary
as our bond seems to be breaking
two citizens of the same city
not relating on topics that used to be shared conversation
a mutual mess we made through disagreements
petty at that

What can be done?
when all the fun has
come to a cease and we're left
with an order to pick up the pieces
everything needs to mend and heal at some point
I'd rather not let my relation die in a bad manner

What can be said of that?
done for that
as a fact, I would rather have the remedy
If I'm not too blind for my eyes to see
as I dust our interaction for signs of prevention
and manipulation...
I'm sure that whatever it is
that eating away at our friendship and kinship
I'll find it and fix it
that's a must for me without maybe's and if's
oh, how much it means and hopefully it felt like that
on a mutual two-might way street
please don't take it lightly
I'm sure it might be better if I asked it
I just pray my methods aren't destructive
I don't want disaster in the bond I'm building
rebuilding what might have been destroyed

DATE OF RELEASE

Days ticking away
ticking away
second by second
minute by minute
as the aging process doesn't stop
I also do not stop

Patience...

Maturity and wisdom
gained in my time waiting
relaxing by thinking of new ways to show it
let others know I have it
all a continuous test to self
as I'm being patient
for my date of release

SOMEONE TO BELIEVE IN

I made a promise to become someone to believe in
so you can have one less enemy
one more friend
putting the nonsense off the table and out the door
so you can be sure of better dealings
and certain of better outcomes
interacting with me plus time for fun
maybe now I won't be so harsh making tempers spark
I can try to remain content with peaceful intent
and see where that gets me
as well as our whole situation
it's all for the best
growing into what you need to see me be
I made a promise to become someone to believe in
we would be happier with less enemies and more friends
I would rather we look at each other with admiration
it's safer and easier than being at each other's throat for nonsense
haunted by ghosts of conflict
chased by the pain inflicted
guided by mistrust
and living life as combative heathens
so I stand by my promise
and instead of arguments, I become someone to believe in

A GIFT

Girl there's something I want to give ya
it's my lifetime I want to share with ya
things wouldn't be right without your gentle hand in mine
coolly combined
ecstasy from the moment we touch
and as we intertwine
I'm more sure of this feeling you give me
its reality
so much stronger than just hope inside
being with you has me walking with a new stride
as I look up the stars are brighter in illumination
and the earth has changed rotation
now the world revolves around us
and our magical time spent together
you need to know
I'm down for you
whenever
wherever
nowadays I can't see it any other way
just how it needs to be
you've shown me what I needed to see
I want you so bad now
my heart bleeds
got me open to this love thing
without you I'm probably lonely and confused
wishing for conversation
praying for emotional interaction
but keeping to myself until the day I met you
you deserve the best of me
and you know that you do
so I stand by my feelings
becuz I know that they're true
if I haven't won your heart yet
I'm yearning for the next clue as how to
woman
that's what you do to me
if it's a game
you're winning
we can share forever
this is just the beginning

I can be with you a thousand years with no fear
my tender mercies are for you alone
you're the destiny for which I've roamed
wondering how deep is your touch
holding a tight clutch on my mind
wanting you to be all mines

coming back home to you in a straight line
finding a new reason to love you every time
sometimes I'm overwhelmed
with the feelings you give me
just so I can release the tension with a sweet kiss
on your honey spot so it's never a miss
all outside thoughts get dismissed
relaxing the mood so we can
get comfortable with this
lovely dipped rubdown got us into something exotic
always time for something erotic
for infinite between the two of us
never finished
each time building for something more glorious
so we can show love for what it actually is
knowing it's that good thing
that taste of heaven
that's what you bring
being with you
now I know what a relationship actually means

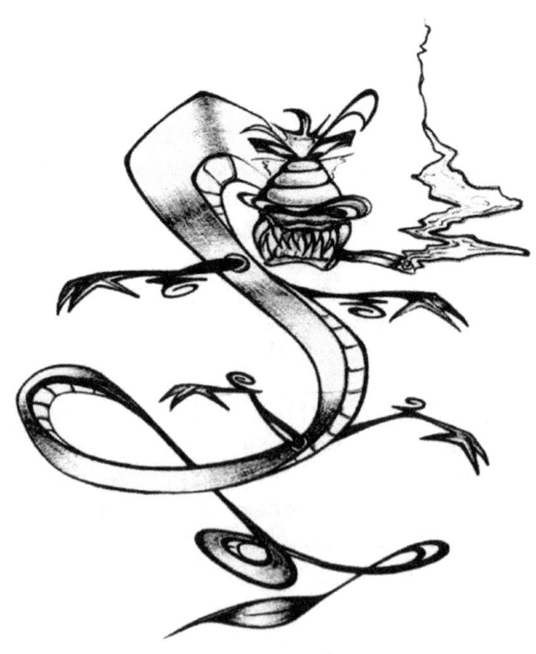

ALL THESE EXPRESSIONS

Coming up with new ways each day
to make words stretch out productively for years
call it what you will
never mind the skill
all this writing has to be good for something
as situations collapse
I document making it evident
that there are adventures for each day
hopefully as far as I can see
I'm making due with the eyes, ears
pencils and paper given
noticing when a soul gets stolen
even more so when the body gives chase
oh and there's a story to tell about it
keeping poetry in a camel clutch
just so the outside observer can get a grasp
at what is being shared rhythmically never scared so umm...
kill at will if...
I didn't pay my dues or pay the bills
there's not a thing but time on my hand
with words on my mind yet I'm not a talkative one
it's an odd combination for a person to be trapped in
seeking new ways to describe it all
for the sake of having something interesting to say
blazeh... hope I'm not a bore... I'm just
being phallic obsessive with the length
of my writings and quotations
lengthening all these expressions

Punctuation means devastation to a run-on sentence
I'm still trying to organize these expressions
so much for worrying where the exclamation points go now...
that's poetry from the soul
with an overabundance of words to make you grow
holding them all in is now charging a toll
back to the free flow
free express without a need to be anything more or less
holding close to the spin of this
like a jewel from a treasure chest
expressions and words stretched to keep me going
going... going... gone
is my mind trying to hold it nevertheless
I'm still standing by like a backup quarterback
I let the poem run its play
crash course to its goal no matter the point across
stretching out with an ease of transition
into the next group together and formation
all these expressions

WHERE THE THOUGHT WENT

As thoughts explode in machine gun burst multiples
the continuous collisions that are reminiscent of the big bang
are more than just a theory
glorious to see and behold
as I carry on with this stroll through the wondrous...
magnificent... wait... hush...
What has become of the thought for the day?
it seems to have disappeared with the wordplay of the hour
you should've seen it
hourglass shaped fitting for the eyes and lips
luscious to have the thought spoken
but the thought was spoken for so...
Was it stolen?
Or maybe kidnapped?
it was nevertheless carried off with the riff-raft
so now the thoughts tainted
painted to perfection it was
golden in its adolescence
now just mundane
described thoughtlessly by a schizophrenic
it was at one time a prize-winning debutante for the ball
but now broken down to a sleazy limerick
maybe that's where the thought went

I thought it went one way
so I chased it only to find myself
running into a wall of writer's block
hands cocked
ready to fight
but the thought was far beyond and out of site
trekking its way to a new destiny
ducking a prewritten eulogy
finding out on its own if it's made of the right stuff
but the last time I saw it
puffed up angry that we had to make interaction
forgetting it was once part of my verbal faction
it's once grand luminesce now broken down to a fraction
had to be knowing that
it's oh so late R.I.P. would be coming by me
the birthright still so new for the death to come into view
and the once wonderful thought
paid its toll throughout its journey
such a fantastic life lived even with its pain and suffering
but alas...
goodbye to the young and worrisome
even somewhat heaven sent
never understanding where the thought went

I WAS CAUGHT UP

I was caught up in the governmental brainwash trap
that is...
I thought this life they provided
with a locked cell was all that was left
institutionalized is what I was being made to be
they called me gravely disabled and violent
kicking it to me like their psyche meds were heaven sent
to the extent that they forced their drugs intake
enemy and prisoner of the state
where oh where did my freedom go?
taken away on the day I stepped into this incarcerated hellhole
got me stuck rubbing my belly like a treasure troll
the only left is to tell me I'm never going home
I'm a convict hence my disdain for C.O.'s
clutching to my last ounce of soul
as well as my visions of free
trapped and the walls are talking to me
segregation and hole shots are all that I got
upping my security level
I hope now I make it to my single cell lifestyle
to finish my bid
damn how many years I put in
positioned into thinking that the outside world
doesn't have anything for me
How grand will my return to it be?
knowing that damn...
they didn't let me go
I still gotta deal with parole
post release control

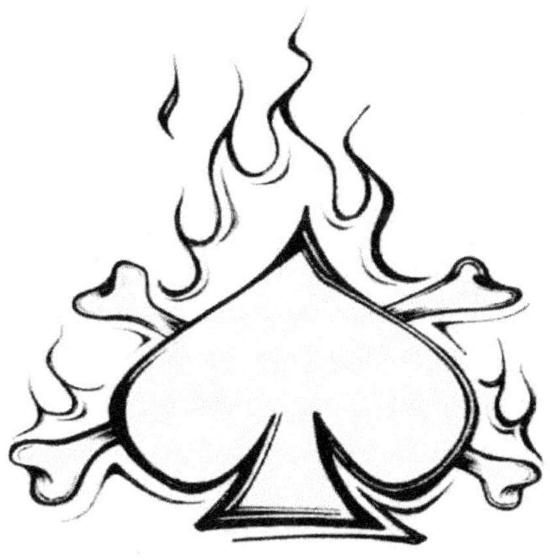

LEAVE ME SOMBER SOLO

They say love the one you're with
Is there always a season for this?
so many times
a person gets trapped with someone they're forced to be cordial with
got me in a somber mood
trying to make due
making me feel more and more decidedly not free
yet I'm supposed to be
How did my hand get caught in this snare?
forced to share
I was getting along better when I was by myself
no one to my left or right
all alone without spite
to take my goods and bads
and face my own downfalls
I can handle a solo pick me up without the disgust
because that's what single entities are made of
so goodbye to the companionships
and I'll hold it down as a monarch for my own grand scheme
for what it's worth
that's what it means
I guess I'll find my way with solitude...

Still in a somber mood

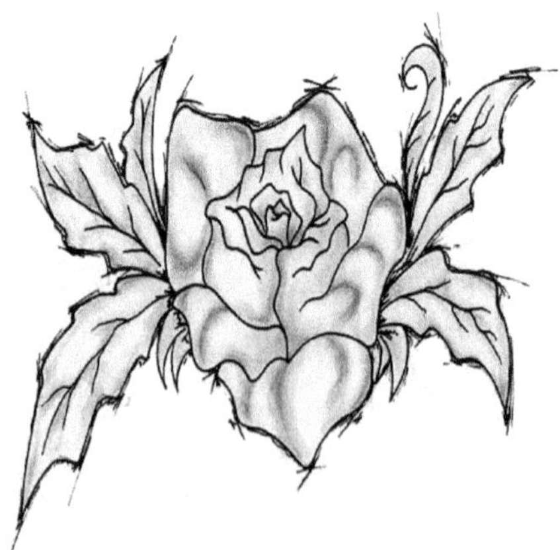

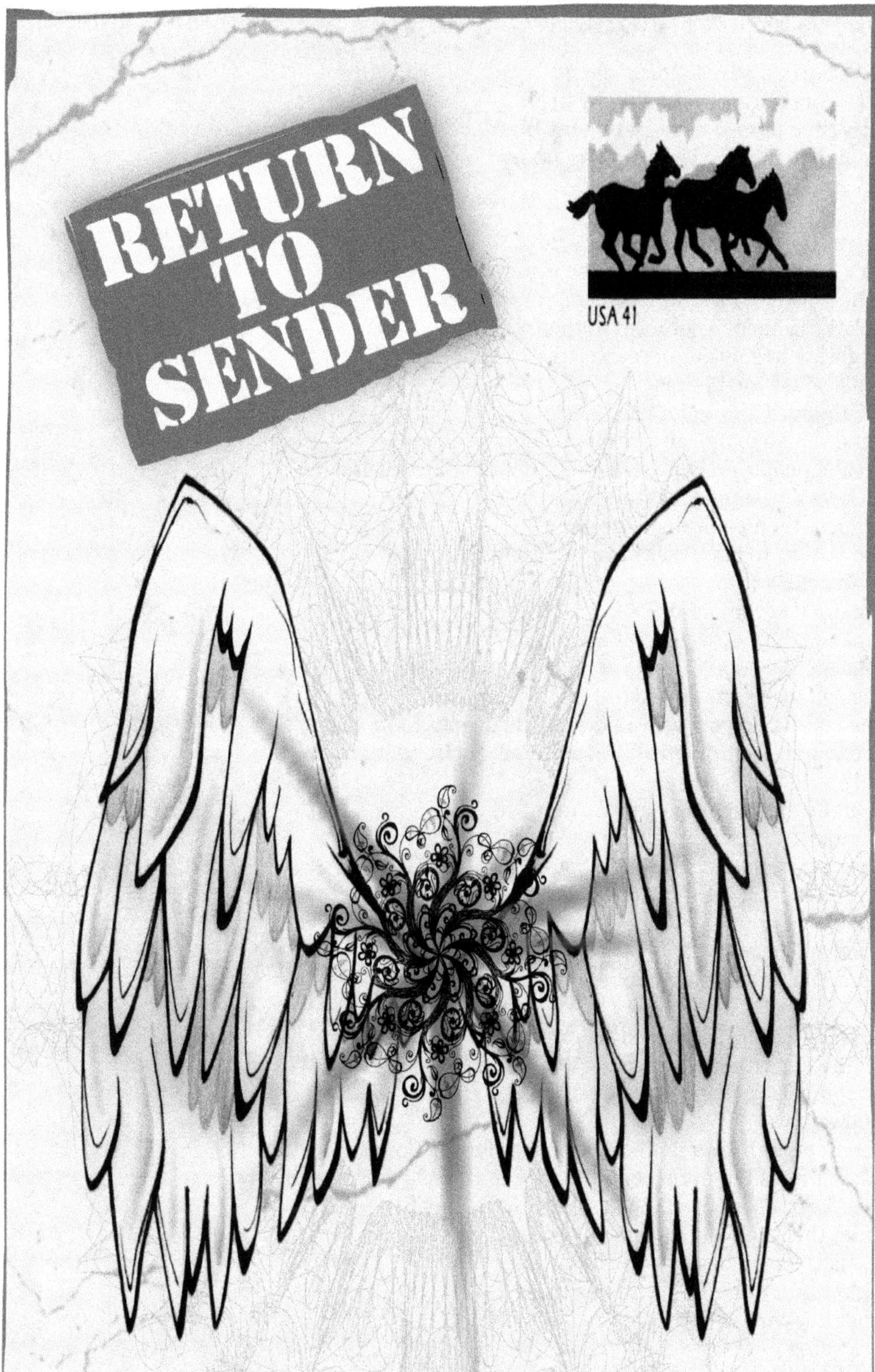

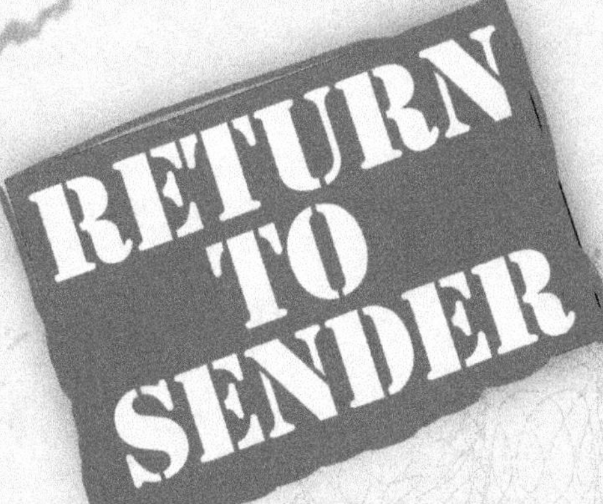
RETURN
TO
SENDER

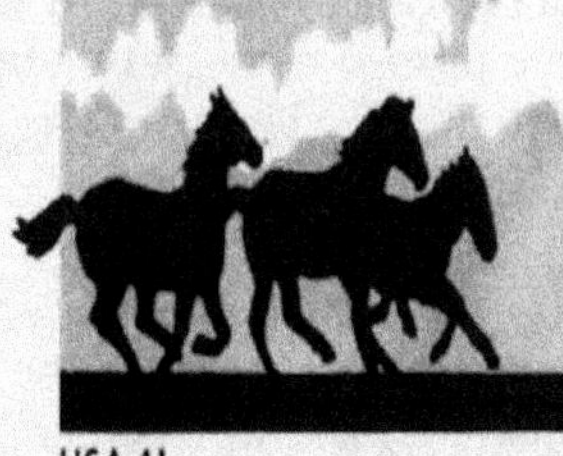
USA 41

I WASN'T AN ANGEL

Concertina wire holding me in
the concrete can't do it all by itself
my time passed by chiseling my mind
so I dive into my writings and books
everybody got a story to tell
just like on the streets
everybody's got a ceedee for sale
it's hard to break away and be different
the reason for so many clicked up soldiers
working hard to conform to the frontline
fighting to stay out of reach from the flat line
that's just what life is
with more drama for each day
and the mixed up government clouding the way
paths people embark on taking them to more dismay
a select few make it through
rich to their capitalistic dreams
to be able to have the things we all need
suits clean...
pressed at the seams
maybe they know what it all means
maybe they don't
I can't dwell on it though
as I'm digging my grave hole a little deeper than usual
cuz I'm reflecting on all this without my freedom in tow...

But I wasn't an angel and I knew this
before I stepped into incarceration
got me trapped
mind
body
and spirit
praying for the day they set me free

Hands aching from holding onto these prison bars
halfway through my stretch and I'm still stuck
hoping for a change in the laws
nowadays
contemplating a rebuild in a society falling down
sometimes I'm not feeling the idea of them letting me go
How am I supposed to work within the means?
and the whole damn systems broke
what I look like stuck on these streets
like a wanderer in a complex mess
not knowing if there's a way out of it
clinging to words I feel
even though they're full of despair

as I'm steady drifting away like steam in the midnight air
my battle mentality going with
I guess I won't be happy until I'm laying down stiff
thoughts spinning dizzy in my head
until the day they let me go
if they won't...
they damn sure better let a brotha know

But I wasn't an angel and I knew this
before I stepped into incarceration
got me trapped
mind
body
and spirit
praying for the day they set me free

Getting dragged by the leash of the governmental beast
convicted by a system of rule
that is only beneficial to a select few
fighting my way to escape poverty
speaking on it without a voice
trapped by my status of being a felon
I guess that's how the lopsided ball bounces
with not much more in my corner
hopefully the next time around
I can stand a little bit stronger
when they decide to stroke me on my sentence
making my way through systematic attitude
and sometimes abuse
my time spent is time I won't get back
to hell with it
let the world collapse
I wasn't the one holding it up
although time in here made me feel
like that was my goal or mission
that's how stressed
with time stretched into a fine line
that thin line between love and hate

But I wasn't an angel and I knew this
before I stepped into incarceration
got me trapped
mind
body
and spirit
praying for the day they set me free

IN THIS CELL

All alone in this cell
a closed in hell
tucked away in a distant place
quiet
but my setting isn't placid or serene
How do you describe something that is unbearable, discreetly?
I guess...
being locked up
is supposed to make my attitude meek toward society
so goes crime and punishment
it's surprising to find how much energy is spent on it
trying to make a humble being out of an individual
by rearranging the lifestyle of an entity
the outside world isn't so great
so I'm looking forward to changing things
let's start right here
no more fears or tears
How many kicks does it take to get things going the right way?
as what I'm focused on comes into view
let me mind my P's and Q's
so I don't repeat what got me in bad placement again
like time is my friend
and as if...
I don't have more important things to do than
sit on a bunk singing the blues
What's a brotha to do?
anything I want
as long as I can get it off in confines of my solitary surroundings
trying to come up with something genuinely astounding
as I watch time slowly float by
sitting in this cell...
this godforsaken hell...

HEY BUTTERCUP

Hey buttercup
I wasn't thinking about a pre-nup when you stepped up
I'm tied tight to our oral agreement in a kiss
and since I haven't witnessed a grievance
I presume it's safe to assume you weren't
at me for material things I can bring
love is naturally a crazy thing
it keeps us open with soul connections
the interaction that isn't store bought
but more so spiritually made
as for me...
I'm a sucker for love
from the cradle to the grave
so serious
with this we build bonds
keeping us closer to each other
as the world moves on
in time and space
each step closer to you gains more grace
relationship so solid we can make
a home out of this place
on the good foot like it's a game to be aced
with you on my arm and I'm more upbeat
the feelings you give me are unique
how much so
to love you forever is my goal
and you already let me know
with you it's the same
so I understand now
that we're alike in mind frames
so I'm cool headed in expressing
just to let you know

A COOLER APPROACH

I'm not sure of the streets I'm coming home to
but I'm sure...
I'm here...
with death near
so a cooler approach to life is something I shouldn't fear
I gain more ground by aging peacefully and gracefully
than I can by bucking against
just about everything
so goes my release to the streets
no longer a victim to the effects I've reaped
so I can't say I'm in too deep
new day
new melodrama
hopefully reacting to it much calmer
than times of old
anticipating the response to my story
when it's told
How will I be portrayed?
Meek or bold?
it won't matter as much as my react in person
I know I'm just a man searching
when I look
finding what I need to see
knowing the truth is still within me
I understand how to deal with it now
making me stronger at peace
accumulating more ways for tension to ease
nowadays not rejecting life
just throwing away the strife
that's something that can be done by me
I'm not sure of the streets I'm coming home to
but I'm sure
I've grown
at first somewhat reckless
this next time around
holding my own

REFLECTED

YOU MAKE ME WHOLE

Loving you so hard
I'm scarred
attached to you like some sticky glue
I'm warm inside too
like a good swig of wine on a winter day
no more dismay
my doubts have been overtaken
by thoughts of your sensuous embrace
love has prevailed this day
I long to be made into an object of your affection
like potter's clay
and may I say
I tingle at your touch
oh so much
I hope the tickle is infinite forever in your grip
it's now golden rhythmical the way my heart skips
back on track a pace
I love your style and your taste
got me sprinting to your side
like I'm in a helluva race
yet you're...
still oh so calm
like a gentle breeze sway
making my day
cooling my way
shining to me like a sun ray
Shall I stay up close so you can read my soul?
my feelings inside
I want to let you know
let me intertwine without interrupting your flow
steady as the ocean waves roll
you heat me up when I'm cold
like a gift given wrapped in a bow
your affection is precious
and you make me whole

SIPPIN' HOOCH

Hooch wine
liquored up
got me on high beams
with a creative mood
lurking through lyrics
finding words often in descript
of my present situation
mind racing
as I settle in a zone
non-sobriety has the best of me
and for now
that's a good thing
constructive ideas are tantalizing
so I steady myself into a laid back pace
easy going with thoughts
having more heat than Tasers and mace
there I go again
relating things to a less than passive affair
Should anyone care?

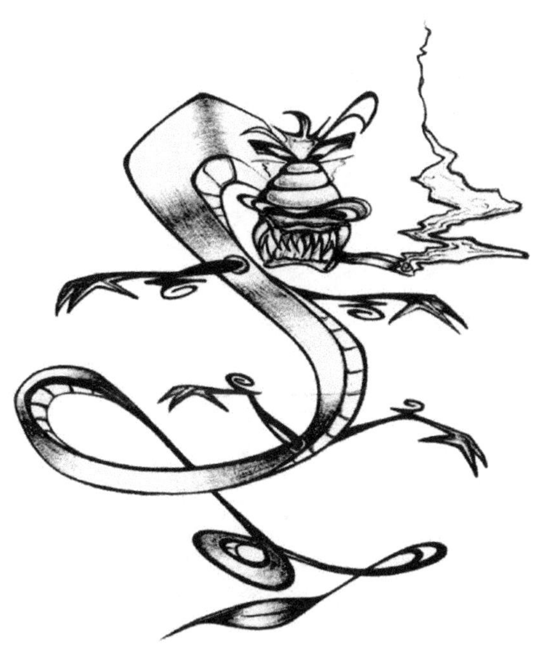

IT WAS MINE TO GIVE

My ballad is my soul's voice reaching with a choice
to the state of nirvana
with or without the pleasure of mirage to guide it
so goes a free spirit
no need of a podium to hold it or hide it
waiting patiently at your listening threshold
for all access to be granted
slave to the slick delivery
topical
heated until it glows
pray the messenger is merciful
fluent in calm tranquility
better for the whole situation
keeping words in justifiable unity
still actively standing in place of an ethereal display
so it was written
all during regular visiting hours
so there's no need to bloodhound about it
originally an organized orgasm
in the mind
ordained to satisfy the spirit
so it's limber
becoming a fixture as it's spoken
invoking a second glance
done out of intuition
disregarding petty reservations about its uniqueness
at times, dizzy with bliss
mission to make the outside world understand
the consequences of this
keep the earth safeguarded during descent
and as the clarity of the whole situation unfolds
the extent of the excursion lingers as a necessary experience
meaningful memory
and a respectable residence
you can keep it...
it was mine to give

SEXUAL

Let me interrogate your lustful mind
so I can find a special spot to relax at
somewhere deep in your sensual imagination
courting your sexual senses
I take my time tickling your earlobe
and blow gently on your nipples
addressing you lovely lady
as I'm undressing you
arousing you as I'm adhering to
the unspoken rules of etiquette
fitting the situation
we have placed ourselves in together
vibing to one another
as you let me enter your private zone
sacred and wet
you're slight jumpy, ready and set
ignited when we grind and motion towards sex
wanting intercourse
fiendin for it
you're still a little timid
wanting that perfect experience
as we continue...
you're so close to it
accepting the rubdown
it's an oil tipped gift
keeping you hotter than August
with more moisture than a tropical storm
I haven't entered yet
so off with the clothes you've worn
losing the slight grip of composure
evident in your muffled moans
the precursor to your ecstasy
with no rebuke for your involvement
you let enjoyment rule for the time
and for the time you're all mine
as I lick the inside of your feminine thighs
on my way to the honey spot
cook and melt you
when I kiss and nibble those lips
my mustache tickling your clitoris
unmerciful as I go at it
scratching and clawing
you give compliance to me as I play down there
cooling you with ice cubes
got you ready for the stroke
until I flip bipolar...
GIRL... I'm not in the mood!

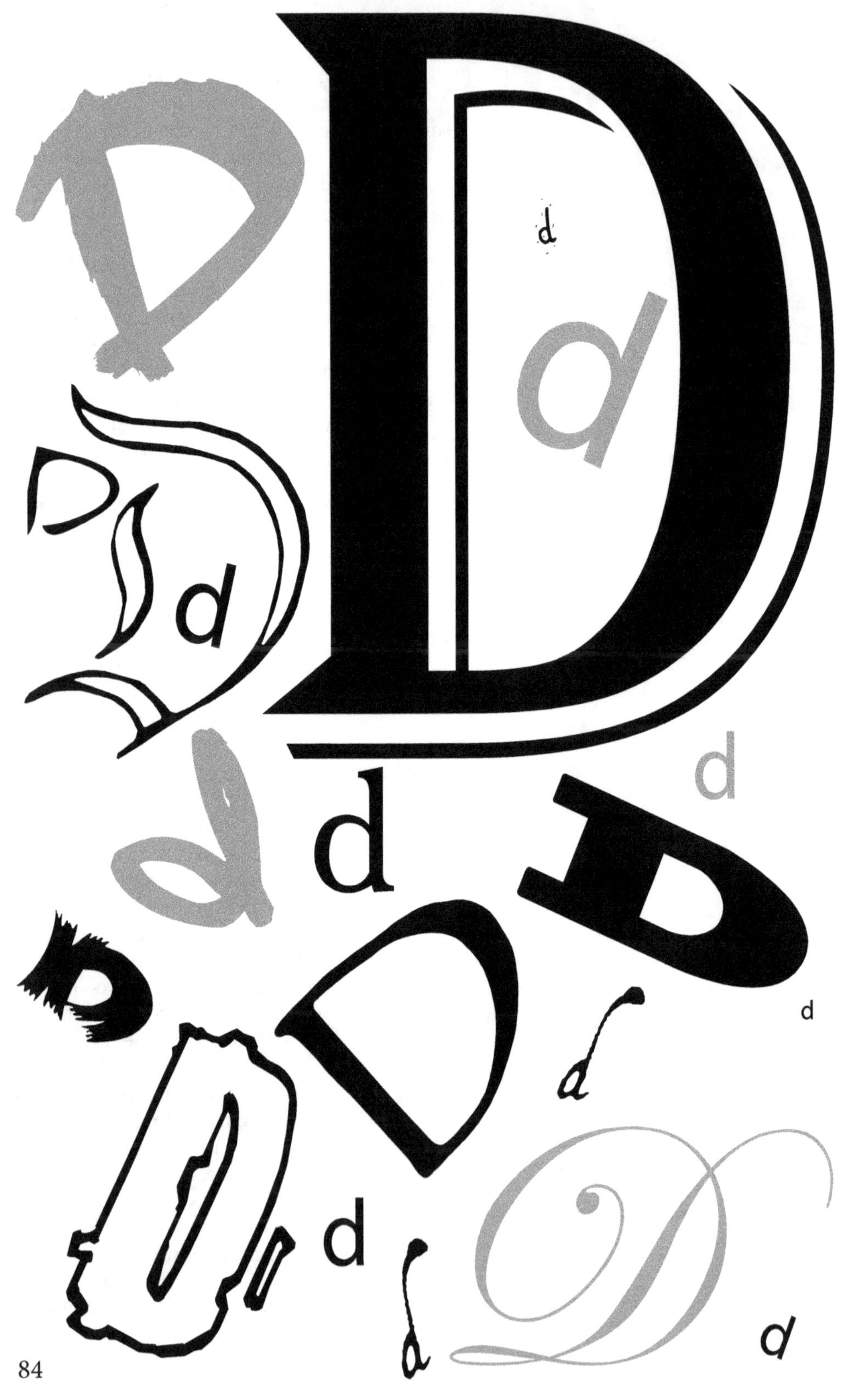

DEALING WITH DEES

Distributing dastardly dew dropping
the disruption directing and dictating
the demeanor of my diary
I dipped into definition
densely dapper is now the
doctrine in my daybook
dealing in a new dawn
defacing defeat
and decidedly defending
delicious descriptions of disclosure
now dominate doses of dreams
as the drama drizzles
I'm dwelling in duty
dwarfing the dwindling dynasty
of dull dissatisfaction
it was disturbing docile discipline
I'm dispersing deliberate dialog
as my deluging demo
denoting the demur denominator
of my delve into discriminate display
due to dealing with dees
do you disapprove?
dispel your dishonor
discover and discuss
discreet diagnosis
of the dynamic devotion
devoid of devious dialect
directed at dexterous diplomacy with dignity
dueling with diabolical discrepancies
devilishly devised...
DAMN!

PRESENTATION

People on the streets got to know me as
that stank bastard smoking cigars
arguing with every thought in circumference
every day a new schizoid alert
but alas...
as all things wear out and fade
so did my outlook
when I stepped outside to look within
come again...
I have enuff juice to leave a circus confused
so I've found on my inner journey
study and you might learn me
but you'd be better off letting the episode just be
one for the strange
to manipulate and wonder
Where can I be tethered?
in a space orbit forever
when it comes to insanity
I have a tight clutch
and it was shown in my persona
so I guess I need some more polish
or whatever you call it
I'm no longer subject to borderline acceptance
becuz spit shine is coming
self continuously
so I can bask in the light of my efforts personally
and unselfishly present the new me...
go figure!

KING OF SPADES

The company I keep is my solo echo
reflecting off the walls surrounding me
I was the King of Spades
with nothing but darkness engulfing
listening to my plea
but the malice in my heart was deafening
firm defiance to my right mind
turning me
slowly into the lunatic tormented
in prolific bursts of outlandish behavior
Where is my so-called savior?
my quickening was too sluggish in its manifestation
my soul slides adrift
my tribulation has no ending
woe be unto all who comfort in this
rage rising within
there is always an antagonist
waiting for an approach
I'm haunted by ghosts of my own creation
dealing in disease of the spirit
erosion of the immortal essence
as the abyss continually calls my name
the outcome
partial insanity with self to blame
deep inside wanting an escape
no longer finding leisure in despair
clutching tightly to everything I hold dear
as loneliness fills the air
I'm off to my personal ruin
waiting for an ending to this private imprisonment

COMFORT ZONE

Regretfully residing in a realm
congested with hell raisers and cell warriors
letting daily arguments pass me by
I don't have much to say
I'm not a child at play
wishing all this was all-good
but it ain't
hoping I could vanish
but I can't

Writing in spite of the raised voices
that come with the surrounding environment
finding ways to relax
even though I'm outside my comfort zone
there's no place like home
my attitude might be doggish
but I'm not Toto
yet I feel like I'm trapped in a kennel

My life...
I wish I could share it with no one but myself
no table talk
I'm too far gone to walk
so I cruise on a cloud
with cloaking abilities
if at all, you barely notice me
I'm already more assertive than I need to be
getting strapped down and drugged up
is my outcome most likely
resting in the mystique
of the myth of rehabilitation

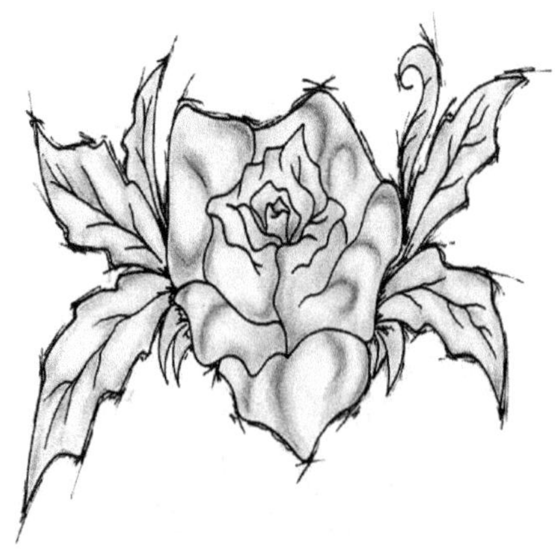

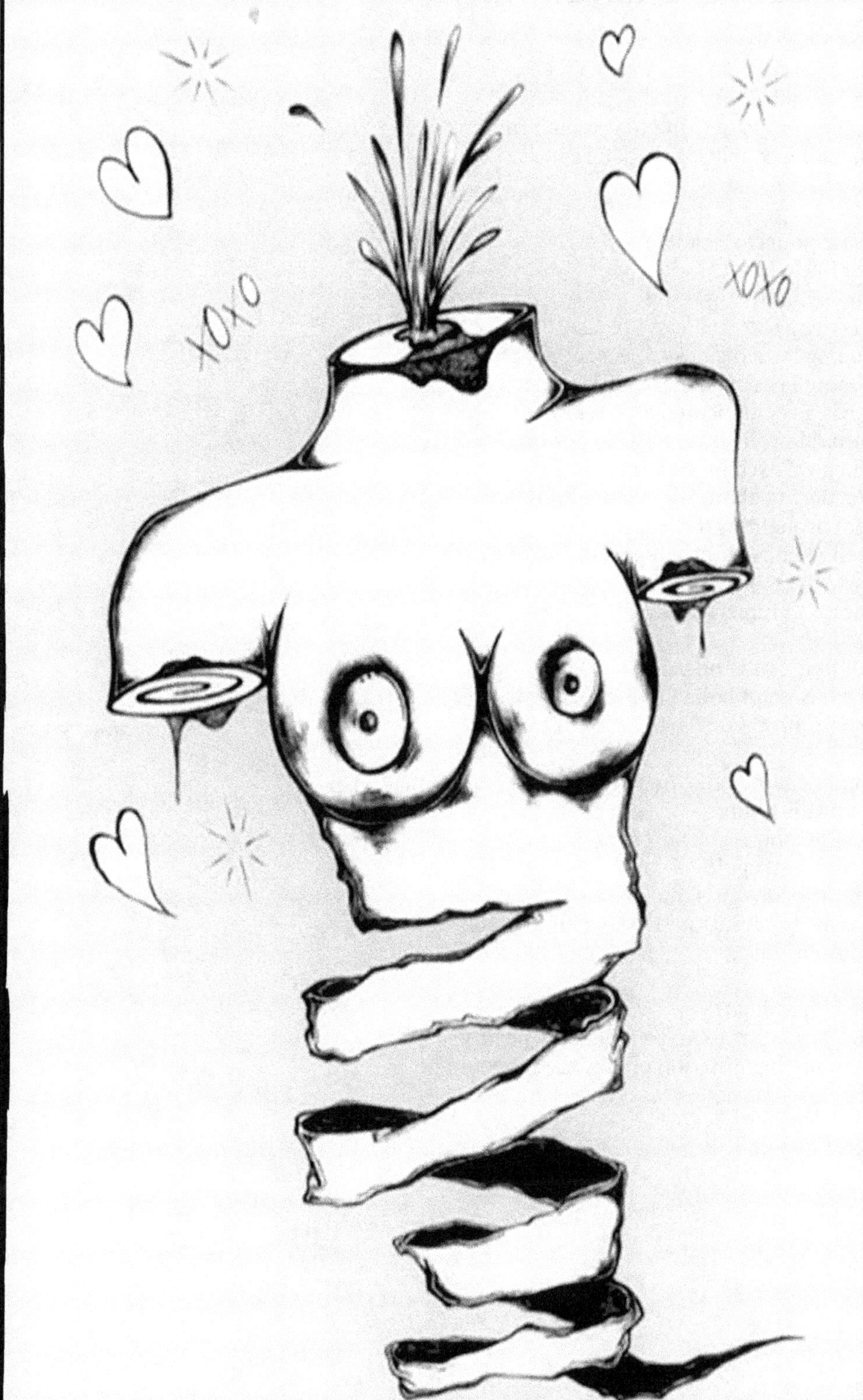
xoxo
xoxo

SHE LOVES ME, LOVES ME NOT

She loves me
she loves me not
so I went insane
hoping for something that wasn't there
watching couples walk before me
paired off...

I'm as lonely as can be
not like a king
but an annoying thing
a court jester that can't please
hoping for a duchess to accept my presence
hoping I can be at ease with a queen
life is as complicated as it seems
I would probably get lost in her eyes
when we exchange glances
wondering about the circumstances
that brought us together
feeling her warmth like a change of weather
can I get to know her?
I want to remember...

All that gloss and sizzle
she has enuff polish to make my life civil
but for now...

I'm unchained like an earthquake of emotion
with this notion
that we should be partners
with no struggle
up close and personal
passively yet intimately sharing passion
without this...

I feel frivolous
so let me refrain myself and stay positive
with my imagination of how things could be
she loves me not...

She loves me!

VIOLENT VANDAL

Lived the life of a violent vandal
too much attitude to be handled
mind state is disregard all of yours
I leave my mark on everything I touch
keeping the public in disgust
as I go about my way content
because I vented
there's no artistic appreciation for this
just messaging
What does it take to consume you in anger?
I'm no stranger to confrontation
vibing off the tribulation I produce
seducing you with the madness I let loose

RELEASING THE MADNESS

Spending a duration of my life
trying to rearrange priorities
I know mistakes are part of me
on an emotional joyride
I'm not perfect
concerned
I reflect on the future and the past
wondering to myself
How long will the anger and depression last?
hoping to erase the sadness and fury
trying to stay busy
capturing pleasure and gratification
making that a permanent occupation
easing and releasing the madness I've known

I WASN'T UP

Graffiti stained walls were always calling to me
I took my time and not the advantage of answering
so I am a lesser of an artist
passing by observing while the culture grew
walking with a can in my hand
balking at the chance to make my name known
in the moving train instead of watching it
while painting on the Redline walls
but then again
what it was never motivated
characters and letters just lost me in a blur
What did it all amount to?
as I survive unseen and growing old
I thought when I was young that it all meant respect
in retrospect
I suppose it's all relevant to something
maybe nothing
I'm already dipping from the force of the law
for more violent things
so let me chill with that
marinating
simmering heat
knowing I probably half-stepped visual art
for the public eye
as I relax with my sketches realizing
they're still privately...
MINE, MINE, MINE!!!

KEEPING BLISS

Everyday a new test
from the same plain
troubled individuals
no rest
souls searching for violence unto themselves
in that case
I'm not here to help
so I keep my anger shelved
for the time being
all around all I've seen is emotional traps
with personas on attack
even with reasoning irrelevant
too much precious spent on it
lives clutching misery wanting to share it, basically
so my catch phrase for the day
is... "keep your distance"
I can find another way
without all that dismay
still knowing
you can't have me
with all you choose to convey
I'm focused enough to make bliss stay

FROM OBSCURITY

Existing in obscurity
anti-socialness has the best of me
you thought it was a phobia
I'm grateful not to offer anything to ya
unburdened with privacy
I remain a self-made reject to the limelight
I'm alright knowing you might never find me
infinite dark tint is my philosophy
paying tribute to tribal outcasts of society
Can we get a humble hurrah?
for the reclusive state of solitude
complementing the mood

FOR LOVE

I would give you the world if I could attain it
I would wipe away all your tears if I were there
if I could bring joy into your life
it would be a mission accomplished
knowing your sadness and helping you get over it
loving you at a distance is something that charges a toll
when I'm not by your side
What does it take to show you that my concern is genuine?
heart spilling out like wine
when you occupy my mind

WHY

Unseen to the naked eye
seek and you shall find
possibly where and what I am
exclusive to a few
greeting you
head on like a running ram
rhythmical body slam
somewhat poetic in touch
not needing too much to spark
creeping through the dark
majestically
burning holes through hearts
it's only a murmur of what I bring
cadence caressing you
while I'm still marinating
fee-fi-foe-fum
Who can comprehend?
And who's accustomed?
wandering through my neck of the woods
like it's all good
I could reject or accept
and invite you to stay and vibe
get you supplied with your fill of funk
for a while
but it might leave you with nightmares
and I don't care...

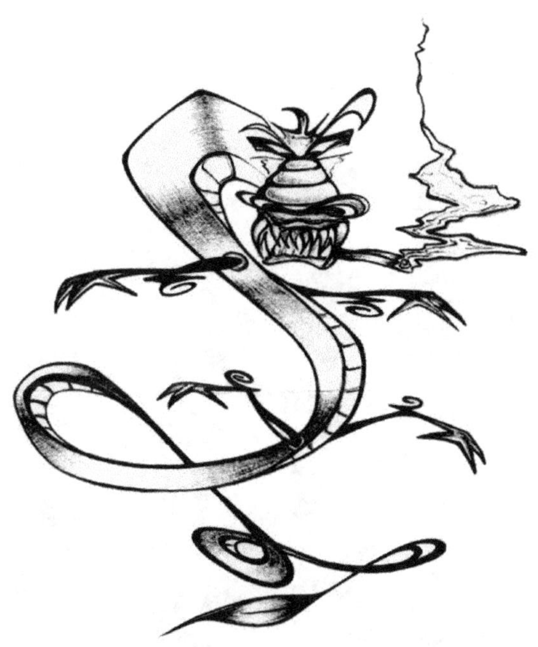

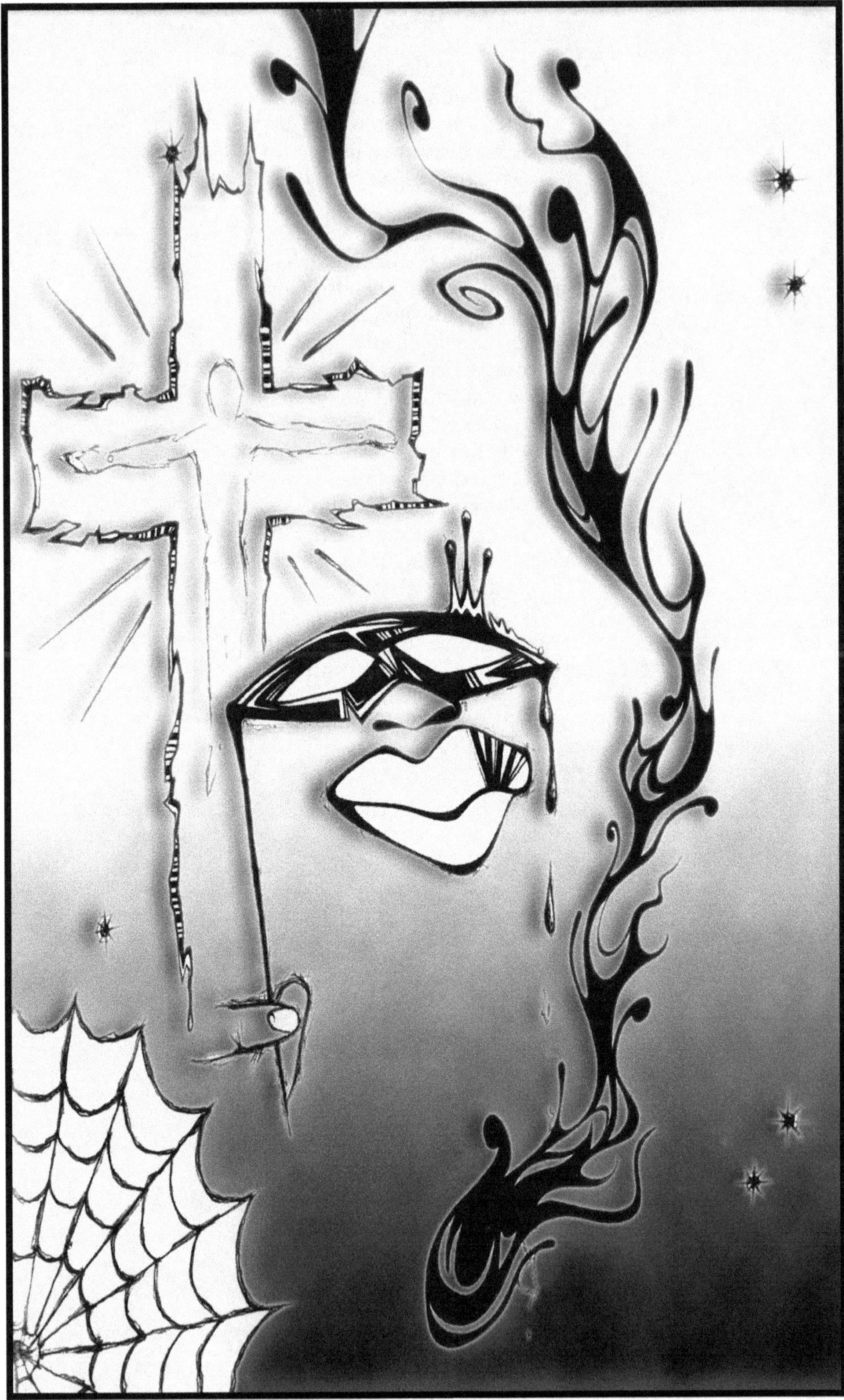

COMPLEXITIES OF LIFE

Complexities of life
the spider's web wove around me
sticky wet lightning
with a burning sensation
no rest...
every time I tried
I was awakened
silver thread keeps me as prey
toyed with while captured
stuck on the dark side of my mind
without an amulet of any kind
to protect me from courting the evil course
of the force that's drilling my soul
lost...
trying to find a way home

AS I EXPLODE

I'm the young black menace battling society
there's no placing me
currently surviving the game
breaking any shackles designed to confine
a cyclone of attitude is adherent
to the swagger I project demanding respect
attracting tension like a magnet
far from being worthless
you just can't handle my limits
I'm the initiator and the conclusion
the escalation will leave you bruised son
with no exception to the rules
I'm evolution of the threat
you knew years ago
and chose not to acknowledge
I shed tranquility during my journey
back to reality
overcoming mores that you people
in mainline society are stuck with
flowing in everlasting like liquid
mortality knows nothing of me
as you paced awestruck I erased it
you must be dumb with bad luck
trying to oppose
with no complexities I rose
keeping a panoramic view of the whole

AS I EXPLODE
Suppressed savage mentality
has its release and season within my reason
you can't comprehend amid the calm group
you choose to circulate with
not knowing the extent of the fire
blazing through the firmament
it's a given that I tend to this you don't want it
while I exist one with the heated spirit
you ducked away from it and I stayed numb
free on a level of climax and nirvana
reading its properties like an encyclopedia
greeting the haze
half-amazed by the sensation it gave
my attitude changed
torching everything in the way
and still walk slowly through inner peace
pleased with the passion
interlocked with my soul

AS I EXPLODE

LIGHT OF DAY

Simmering with a hangover from a fantastic fantasy
the light was with me
perfume scented
pleasingly
I was happy to assist and receive its coming
carrying on elated
never mind the tardy afterthought of being self-conscious
with a gift
more pep in the step
keeping the episode moving
for a delightful trip
I was taken to another zone
the luminance got me high on its own
steady in flight
I glide
meeting destination X as I kiss the sky
please pardon the parlay
the event was heavenly
the type of incident we all need continuously
making it the entrée to consider when an entity searches
always
the aura for which we take chances
greeting it should it ever come again
that shine from the light of day

HIATUS

Handcuffed hiatus
getting the best of me
hating everything
daydreaming of heinous deeds
socializing like a hand grenade milking time
moments before the sudden burst
agitated first
ready to disperse anger
making the whole area a disaster

STATEMENT FROM SURVIVAL

Statement from survival in a spot
where killers dwell
defiance in hell
the nightmares are in splinter cells
vicious and carnivorous
lurking in the abyss
attracted to the torchlight
not concerned with what is wrong or right
taking refuge in the depths
refusing help
impatiently examining the essence of all who approach
devouring any who encroach
deliberately lounging in the killing fields
the conflict of conforming is real
wondering if fate was already sealed
roaming on the road of emotion
knowing fortune might bring ruin
holding grace
instead of being timid
staying headstrong and dealing with all of it

WHAT THEY WANTED

Lives in jeopardy
becuz of ideas about national security
heavy friction and soldier placement
all eyes focused on the signs of world war
your casket is calling and waiting
countries anticipating the fallout and more
rifts and conflicts are never finished
death and sorrow won't have conclusion any time soon
while world leaders steady seal our doom
Who's to rebuke?
somber is the attitude of the voiceless in war torn environments
Can leaders relate to that?
media outlets still hiding the facts
military generals calling for troop movements
overlooking the land's inhabitants
rank commanders catering to the fetish of occupation
territories submitting to hostility and overt force
no time wasted
no second-guessing the harsh course
so much blood spilled over unproven ideals
getting exactly what they wanted from the average man's anger
a time to kill

CONFORMITY

Abiding by the unwritten rules of a violent world
adjusting to comfort as needed
society is conceited
with bleeding hearts for the privileged
scared with a bunch of double talk
heard discussing money matters
fine wine
and calling the shots of which soldiers get popped
in corporate backed wars
currency culprits
financial whoredom
on international levels
conforming to the ways of the devil
it's a narrow path to tolerate all this
and still keep hold of soul
in the fallout and aftermath
small countries get manhandled
when opposition is shown
pledge allegiance as a child
becuz as adults you should've known
the powers that be
peddling death penalties to every continent they roam
What you gonna do now?
if you can't make it on your own

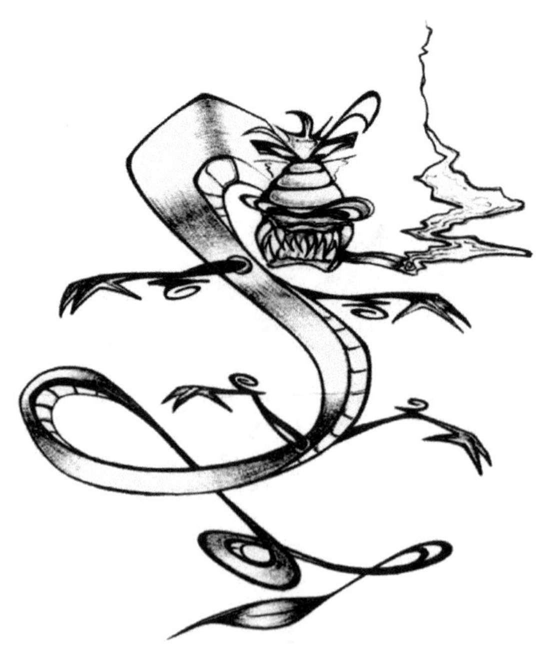

TAGGER

Walking around brick canvas
there's a tension with not being seen or discovered
silence was the word I uttered
Who made the blank space?
be happy I'm anti-social
absorbed more by thoughts in my inner skull
working metro city streets
that know me more by my signature
not a picture
absolutely more a vandal
less an artist
so fear your property's well-being when I roam
rolling stone without a home
I'm on my own
thick black markers
documenting pathways I've traveled on my journeys
still with that
I don't need you to know me
introverted while the rest of the crowd
runs about colorful and large scaled
my viewpoint of the art scene isn't well received
yet I keep it close to me
there's no need to label my persona with deceit
that's only your oneself duel
your oneself duel its only
choose to ride
tag along
I control what you see in my coming
inner city sign-offs
essential to the well-being of society
You not believe?
then it's just changing and defacing things
that tickles my fancy
tagging my way through urban landscape's
future and history...

BIG TALKERS

Enduring crusades of big dreams
big talking got me watching to see
which ones will live it up
and stay true to what they converse
sometimes it hurts to think they might not achieve
but it's annoying to hear some carry on
like they're actually committed experts
on every topic that's in reach
some people have mouths
and talk like they're beasting the whole scene
some have attained every excuse
to give a crutch to their stories
nowadays I've learned
not to trust everyone and everything
everything...
some people will say anything about everything
making listeners cynical about every dream
please address the terms 'humble' and 'humility'
please at ease
all that boasting is making ears bleed
big talker!

LUCASVILLE BLUES

Institutionalized
frozen young mind
another stat trapped by the myth of rehabilitation
another brotha's life wasted
waiting to be terminated by the powers that be in control
so many years stole
again and again
reawakening agitated tension
that was trying to settle

The path of freedom...
blocked by bars of heavy metal
billy clubs and gun towers
in a place where the weak get devoured
mentalities get readjusted by the cold surroundings
then they exist more abrasively
not an ideal place to be

District attorneys know very little
of the other side of the walls and fence
continually pushing for the maximum sentence
public defenders scared to rebut this
so a margin of our population stays stuck and caught up
in the mess that was made of the judicial system

Nobody warned them
and for more than some
nobody remembered the children

Leg shackles and handcuffs
are the modern day lynch noose
slowly suffocating generations
no more room to breathe
no more space to release
nothing left but caged rage and anger
torching the mirage of a world at peace
thoughts of tranquility gone
as reality gets erased to caged emptiness

DRAMA QUEENS

Telepathy tells me there are drama queens lurking around
gossiping bound
to set off explosions of incidents
physical because of the here say
smashing comfort zones
penetrating personal space
dipping in the unknown
never resting their case
only made content when more friction unfolds
when there's someone else to loathe
so the attitude stays cold
so the situation stalkers can knit pick
with something to hold boldly dancing around
playing with the fire they were warned about
so many times
Who's sexing who?
Who's in jail and who died?
childish games from grown-ups with evil intent
be warned
find a way to disappear
if you had enuff of it
hopefully it's a good suggestion

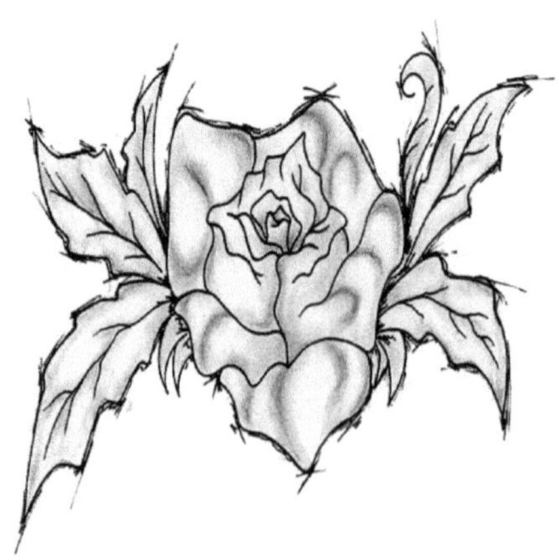

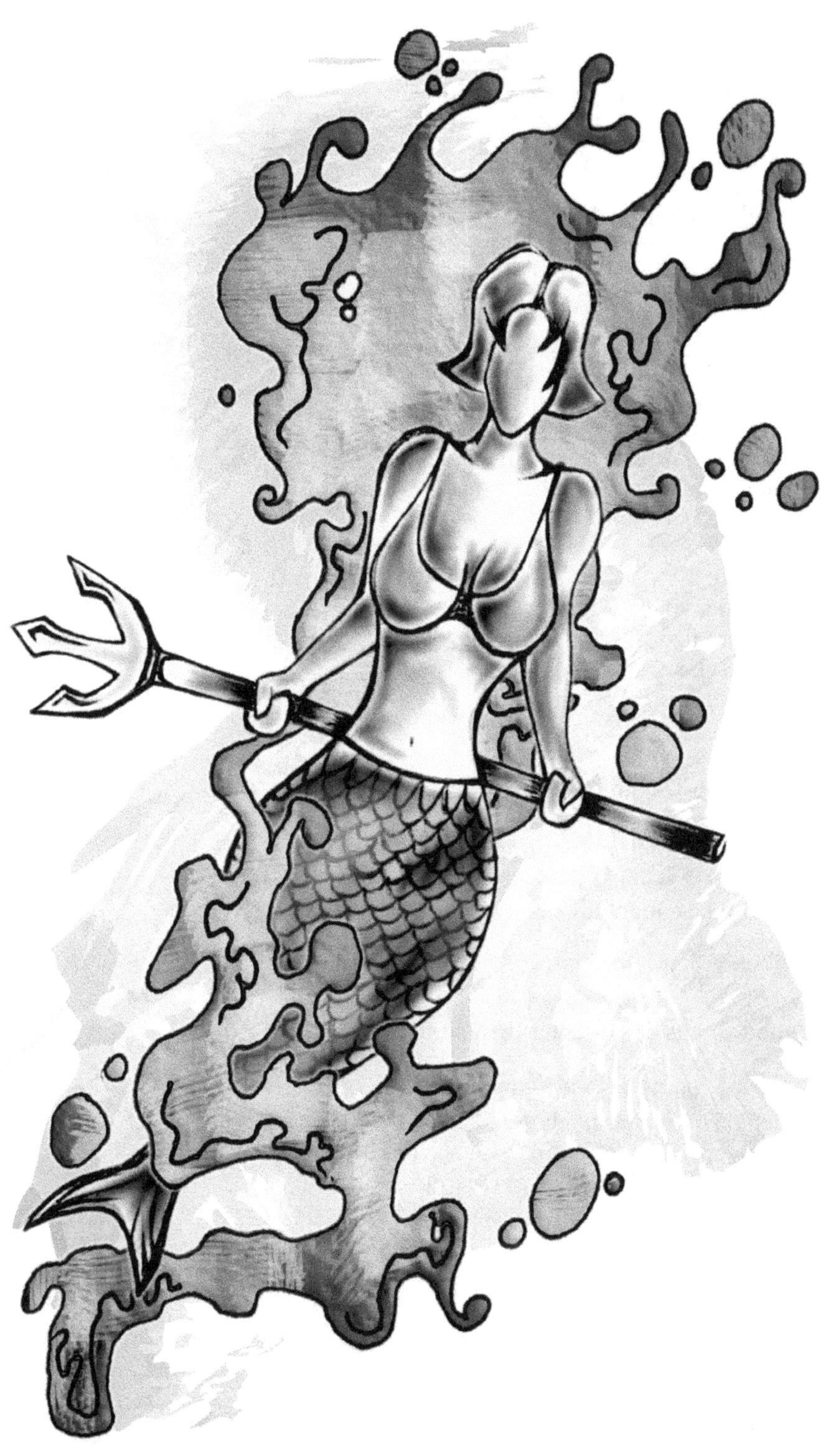

MERMAID AND THE VAMPIRE

She had aquatic grace
her approach was confident and smooth
her heart in full bloom could heal nations
yet I felt part of her was left disdained
after our interaction and encounters
I should've warned her that my heart
was dark like a night without the moon
and she was modest when she told me
she had a lot of love too

Selfishly
I wanted to siphon all of it
more power and support as I live
and none to give
keeping her like a close pet for my purposes
even though I knew she couldn't exist the same
not without her freedom

She's not dumb
I marauded her space
a true vampire fiendin for her taste
so I hastened the head games
to swiftly have control of her mind

One of a kind
maybe I underestimated her mentality
the trick was on me
crossing the path of a warrior queen
a water goddess
that could make a man flow with tears so easily

The mermaid had me vexed
when conflict finally arrived
it was good versus evil and her light shined
as I observed and absorbed
her mercy was bleeding through me
she reflected compassionately
eclipsing my misgiven attempt to deface her being
defeating my efforts to control and capture

Her rapture much sharper
than my fangs of affliction
for the first time
I wondered where the sunshine went
and realized she was one with it
I understood it was the glow I missed
now because of her

it encompassed me and I had to accept it
consuming my darkness and I felt it

My world started to change
things of the night now seemed strange
as she made her moves around my step
she showed so much finesse
I was taken back
now accepting goodness
no longer a creature of the dark
the mermaid had a healing

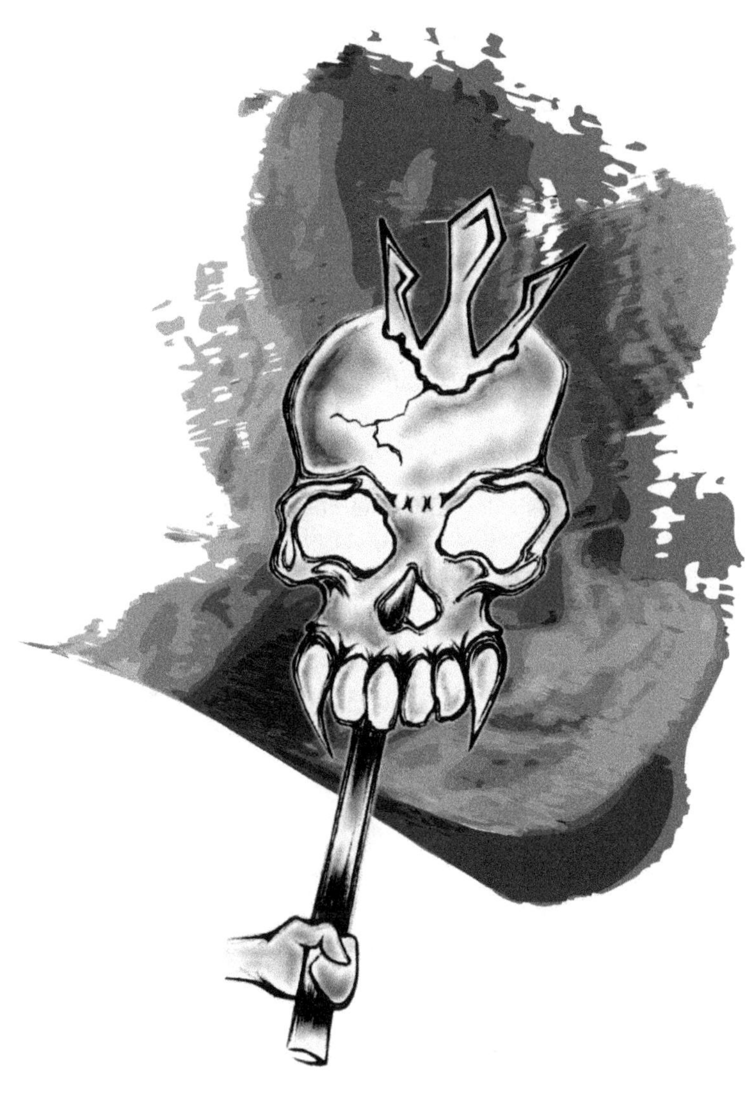

NOT ALL GOOD

Crime and punishment only explains part of it
so much penalizing of the penalties
so little work for rehabilitation outside
they haven't felt the bruises
from the shackles and handcuffs
enuff to make a civilized man stray
How long is the stay?
there's so much stuff behind years of incarceration
aging can't be described by words alone
a ton of letters written home
can't grasp or explain the aching in the mind
the aura of being confined
and vexation of returning to what's outside
the echoing walls and bloodstained halls
What else for the memory to keep?
the release has to be meek
because the prison system retention level
is as high as can be
society detaining society
men
women
children
all the same
not enuff attention to education
so people endure the pain
What's being done with the population?
dangerous games leading to more disarray
disorder and systematic slavery
endorsed like it's all okay

MY TWO CENTS

Made it thru to the other side
breaking everything in the way
my bad
if I had an easier route
I would've saved a little something for the pain relief
migraines and body aches
interrupting study
so I can't pay much attention to yours no more
laugh it off if you're sore
and let me marinate in the wreckage
I promise I can fix it in due time
I'll grant you that very wish
not meaning to be devilish
but if I leave you dazzled
I probably knew I would do this
I thought heavily about leaving the whole scene
un-tampered in bliss
but all stories have a twist
I'm waiting to see
how many times people
let this one get flipped
posted in the center
balanced
while everything gets changed
then comes the defiant rage
emotionally caged
set free for preservation purposes
not everything needs revolution
but if you don't like the final product
find another denomination
because I'm chilling
stuck with my two cents in it
now it's finished

BREAKING THE SOUND BARRIER

Holding my own in a pressure cooker
let me vent before something explodes
tell me it ain't real
you want to know
the depth is lifelong
everlasting
thought the old earth passed long ago
What is it for wisdom to hold?
understanding was the new life for her
to nourish and grow
there's no separation for my young star
no matter how far the moon or the planets
so I'll try to stay righteous
not just for self
but the new brightness that's following
reflecting the glimmer
spotted from a distance
backed by mother's intuition
understanding star coming to a glow of its own
for that I'm wide awake
conscious to the facts and placement of myself
all alone in conceptual meditation
urban relocation
even abstract communication
with a gift not to be ignored
ventured to in all sorts
set for a new heaven to find it
sparking the intellect...

SONIC BOOM!!!

Explore the explosion as your third eye opens

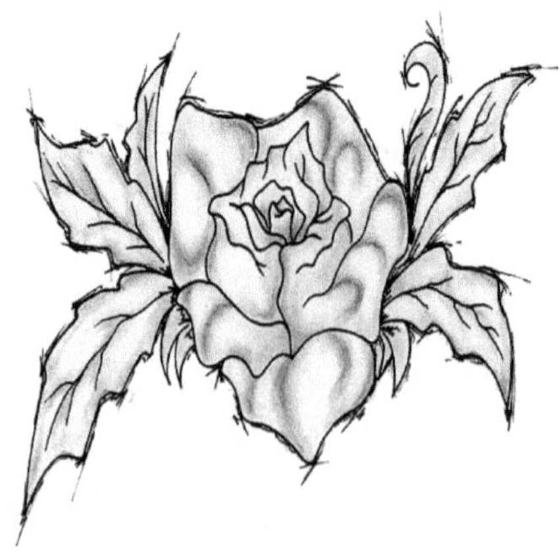

JUST ENTICING

OOOOOO...
there's something that you do
keeps me occupied
eyes locked in on your motion
mesmerized
hurting me with want and yearn
you'd better have an alibi
lovely woman
there's no reason why we shouldn't be together
mingling...

Yeah...
I'm singling you out
without a doubt
I'm seduced by just a glimpse
watching you lick those lips
the curves of your hips

Hey honey dip
you might have me whipped
without too much resistance
I insist on treating you
with something warm and soft

Make it hard on me if you want
mo' better for the pleasure
as I'm getting more sure
for the approach

When I get you we gonna coast
cloud nine
ten
twelve or thirteen
baby I'll make you float
by half past eleven

You ain't met a magic man quite like me
for your eyes only
I fit you nicely
sweep you off your feet
while you're looking

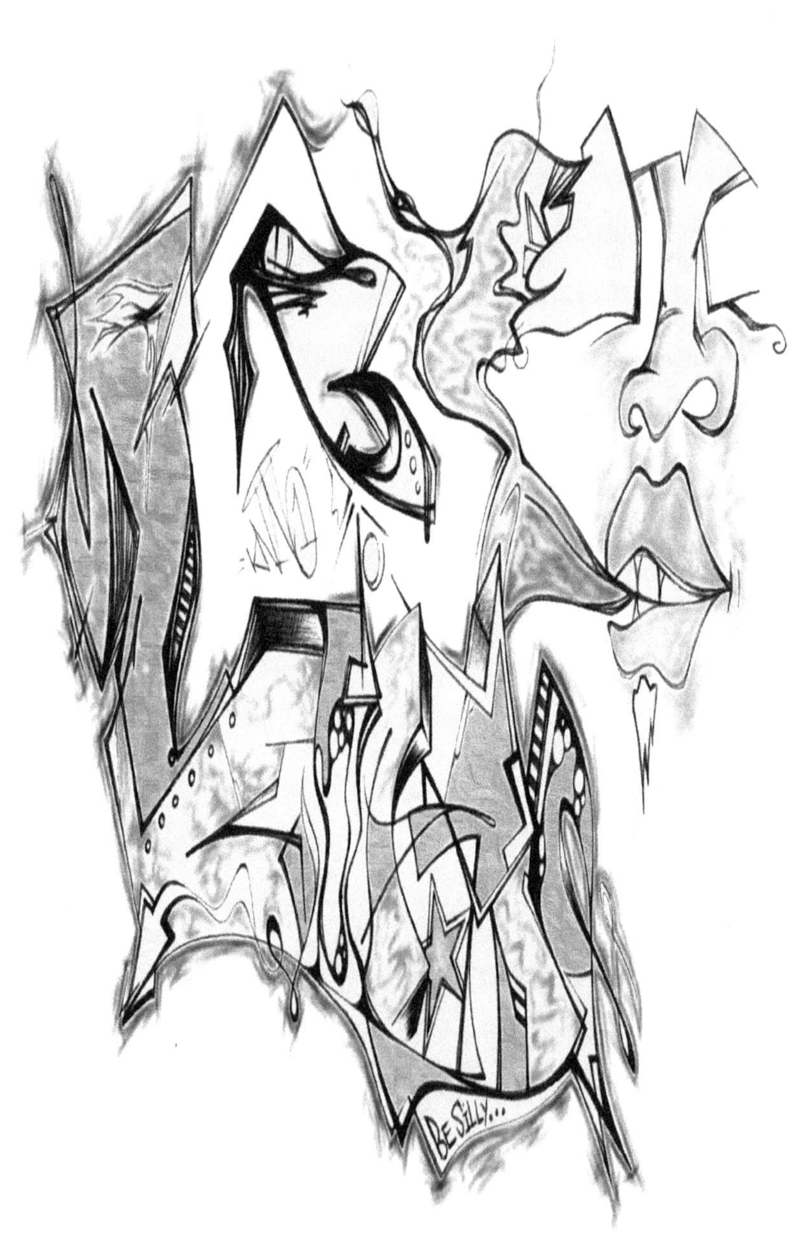
BE SILLY...

www.ingramcontent.com/pod-product-compliance
Lightning Source LLC
LaVergne TN
LVHW010934110826
845149LV00013B/2591

* 9 7 8 0 9 9 1 6 5 3 1 1 9 *